ARAB MiG-19
AND MiG-21
UNITS IN COMBAT

SERIES EDITOR: TONY HOLMES

OSPREY COMBAT AIRCRAFT • 44

ARAB MiG-19 AND MiG-21 UNITS IN COMBAT

David Nicolle and Tom Cooper

OSPREY
PUBLISHING

First published in Great Britain in 2004 by Osprey Publishing,
Midland House, West Way, Botley, Oxford OX2 0PH, UK
44-02 23rd St, Suite 219, Long Island City, NY 11101, USA
Email: info@ospreypublishing.com

Osprey Publishing is part of the Osprey Group.

Transferred to digital print on demand 2011

First published 2004
3rd impression 2008

Printed and bound in Great Britain

A CIP catalogue record for this book is available from the British Library

ISBN: 978 1 84176 655 3

Edited by Tony Holmes and Bruce Hales-Dutton
Page design by Mark Holt
Cover Artwork by Mark Postlethwaite
Aircraft Profiles and Scale Drawings by Mark Styling
Index by Alan Thatcher
Origination by PPS Grasmere Ltd., Leeds, UK
Typeset in Adobe Garamond, Rockwell and Univers

Acknowledgements

The authors wish to thank all those retired and serving officers of the Egyptian, Syrian, Iraqi, Indian and Algerian Air Forces, several of whom are sadly no
longer with us, who gave interviews or provided information for this book. Special thanks are also due to Lon Nordeen for allowing us to quote substantially
from interviews he conducted in the 1980s, to Sherif Sharmi for letting us draw upon his decades of research into the history of his country's air force, to
Yaser al-Abed for interviewing active and retired officers from his country's air force, to Mrs Munira Kafafi and Mrs Khouda Tewfik for facilitating vitally
important interviews, to George Agami for his translations of published Arabic sources, to Tom N for his extensive and irreplaceable help in research and
especially to the 'First of the Last'.

Editor's note

To make this best-selling series as authoritative as possible, the editor would be extremely interested in hearing from any individual who may
have relevant photographs, documentation or first-hand experiences relating to the elite pilots, and their aircraft, of the various theatres of war.
Any material used will be fully credited to its original source. Please contact Tony Holmes at 16 Sandilands, Chipstead, Sevenoaks, Kent, TN13 2SP
or via email at tony.holmes@zen.co.uk

The Woodland Trust

Osprey Publishing is supporting the Woodland Trust, the UK's leading woodland conservation charity, by funding the dedication of trees.

www.ospreypublishing.com

Front Cover

On day nine of the Ramadan or Yom Kippur War (14 October 1973), the Israelis launched a full-scale air assault on several Egyptian air
bases, including el-Mansourah, which resulted in a prolonged aerial battle in which Egyptian MiG-21s shot down several Israeli aircraft.
One of these fell to Lt Mohamed Adoub of No 104 Fighter Air Brigade, who downed an F-4E over the Nile with a series of accurate 23 mm
cannon bursts fired from close range. Perhaps a little too close, for his MiG-21MF in turn suffered mortal damage when it was struck by
debris from his quarry – an Israeli Defence Force Air Force (IDF/AF) Phantom II. Adoub and the surviving F-4 crewman ejected virtually
alongside each other, the MiG-21 pilot subsequently rescuing his injured foe from enraged Egyptian farmers on the ground.

The Egyptian Air Force (EAF) had enjoyed such success on 14 October that its annual EAF Day has been celebrated on this date
ever since (*Cover artwork by Mark Postlethwaite*).

CONTENTS

INTRODUCTION

The history of the Arab-Israeli confrontation is widely-known and widely-misunderstood. This, however, is not the place to go into the convoluted rights and wrongs of a continuing struggle, nor even to offer an objective account of the air wars between the Arab states and what some of their governments still call 'the Zionist entity'. This book tries to tell the story of two Soviet-designed fighters in frontline Arab service and of the men who flew and maintained them under appallingly difficult circumstances. To describe it as a story 'from the other side of the hill' presupposes that the authors and most of their readers will be on the Israeli 'side of the hill', which is of course not necessarily the case.

The first Soviet-bloc combat aircraft purchased by some Arab states was the MiG-15 in 1955, closely followed by the MiG-17. Their story will be told in a later volume in the Osprey Combat Aircraft series. By the late 1950s the arms race between Israel and its Arab neighbours was becoming serious. In 1958 Egypt and Syria joined to form what was supposed to be a single state – the ill-fated United Arab Republic (UAR). In 1961 Syria seceded, although for another decade Egypt continued to call itself the UAR.

The Egyptian Air Force had been created in 1932 as the Egyptian Army Air Force (EAAF), being styled the Royal Egyptian Air Force (REAF) until a military coup in 1952. Not long after that coup, headed by Col Gamal Abdel Nasser, the monarchy was abolished and the air force became simply the Egyptian Air Force (EAF). That title would be restored in 1971 when President Anwar Sadat quietly dropped the name UAR.

In 1960 the UAR (Egypt-Syria) and Iraq began a major effort to improve their air strength, followed a little later by Algeria. This involved obtaining aircraft able to fly faster than sound in level flight, followed by subsequent purchases able to exceed Mach 2. The aircraft in question were the MiG-19 and the MiG-21, although Iraq was also acquiring Hawker Hunters from Britain. Nevertheless, President Nasser's Four Point Plan to confront Israel on seemingly equal terms was only possible as the result of massive arms deliveries from the Warsaw Pact countries, primarily the USSR.

The Arabs' ambition was to build air forces capable of facing the Israeli Air Force (IDF/AF), and this provided a golden opportunity for the USSR to extend Soviet political influence in a region previously dominated by the British.

THE ARABS GO SUPERSONIC

In 1959 Israel acquired supersonic Super Mystère jet fighters from France, and the following year the UAR (Egypt and Syria) ordered the similarly-performing MiG-19 from the Soviet Union. The Middle Eastern arms race was now in full swing, and Egypt initially intended to obtain four squadrons of MiG-19s. Eventually, the UARAF obtained about 80 of these first-generation interceptors, although not all came directly from Soviet factories. The first arrived in the summer of 1961, and comprised the MiG-19S day fighter, with limited all-weather capability, which could also be used in a ground-attack role. Later, Egypt obtained the all-weather MiG-19P or radar-equipped MiG-19PM, although not apparently from the USSR. These may have been among the aircraft transferred from the Iraqi Air Force, or they may have been licence-built Czechoslovakian S-106 versions of the MiG-19PM.

The structure of the UARAF, including its new MiG-19 squadrons, remained essentially similar to the Royal Air Force, on which it was modelled. A supposed restructuring along Warsaw Pact lines remained superficial, with a wing or *jinaah* now being translated as an air brigade. Most comprised three squadrons, each with between 15 and 20 aircraft. The MiG-19 air brigade, however, only ever had two squadrons, and for various reasons these would soon be combined into a single unit.

The first group of Egyptian pilots sent to the USSR to train on the MiG-19 had already flown MiG-17s, and included men who would subsequently become prominent in the UARAF. Four trained as pilot-attack instructors (air-to-air and ground-attack), including Sqn Ldrs Shalash, Ahmad el-Dirayni (who commanded Egypt's first MiG-19 squadron, and who was later killed while fighting Biafran rebels with the Nigerian Air Force) and Magdi el-Miklawi, who died during a MiG-19 night training exercise. Among the slightly younger pilots were Alaa Barakat, Abd el-Moneim el-Tawil and Nabil Shoukry, who went to the USSR in June

Four of Egypt's first supersonic pilots pose in their new high altitude G-suits by the tail of one of the UARAF's newly delivered MiG-19Ss in 1963. They are, from right to left, Maj Alaa Barakat, squadron CO and future Egyptian Air Force chief, Capt Galal Abdel Alim, Capt Farouk Abdel Latif and Capt Abd el-Moneim el-Tawil (*Alaa Barakat*)

One of the UARAF's ex-Iraqi MiG-19Ss lands with its braking parachute deployed on either 20 July or 11 August 1965 (*EAF*)

Four Egyptian fighter pilots walk towards their MiG-19Ss on 20 July 1965. These were ex-Iraqi Air Force aircraft which had the names of Iraqi cities painted on their forward fuselages (*EAF*)

1960. Upon their return, these pilots formed Egypt's first MiG-19 squadron at Fayid, close to the Suez Canal. During a graduation ceremony at the Air Academy at Bilbays in 1961, Alaa Barakat was among the MiG-19 pilots who performed a high-speed flypast to celebrate the formation of Egypt's first supersonic interceptor unit. They broke all the windows in the control tower!

Nasser soon decided that instead of ordering further MiG-19s, Egypt should concentrate on the more advanced MiG-21. Meanwhile, the two MiG-19 squadrons gave the UARAF useful experience in operating supersonic fighters. The Egyptians had hoped to organise a MiG-19 aerobatic team to perform alongside existing MiG-15 and MiG-17 ones, but the aircraft proved unsuitable for such formation flying. Criticisms of the MiG-19 included its steep landing angle, big nose, which reduced visibility, limited range and poor payload in the ground-attack role.

Nos 20 and 21 Sqn soon formed No 15 Air Brigade under Ahmad Hassan Dirayni, while Alaa Barakat took over command of No 20 Sqn. Fayid was the air brigade's main airfield, while Milayz, in the Sinai peninsula, was used as a forward base. In 1964, maintenance problems resulted in the two squadrons being combined into one 'big squadron', apparently renumbered as No 27/29, commanded by Alaa Barakat.

The biggest problem experienced with the MiG-19 was the positioning of the hot air venting pipes, which ran close to the aircraft's hydraulic tanks. Unfortunately, the Russians failed to warn the Egyptians that holes could appear in these pipes and cause fires in the hydraulic tanks. As a result, the combined squadron was soon reduced from 26 to 20 aircraft. Despite such

A pair of Egyptian MiG-21F-13s escort a UARAF Tu-16 heavy bomber, armed with KSR-2 'Kelt' stand-off missiles, during a ceremonial flypast over Cairo in 1965 (*EAF*)

This Israeli gun-camera photograph shows an Egyptian MiG-19 just moments prior to it being shot down by cannon fire over the Sinai frontier on 29 November 1966. The aircraft still has its drop-tanks and two air-to-air missiles beneath its wings (*IDF*)

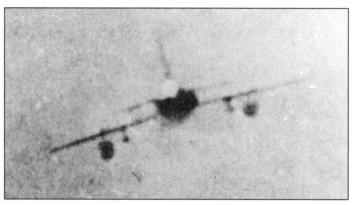

A 'finger four' of UARAF MiG-21F-13s in 1964, probably from the first Egyptian squadron to be equipped with these interceptors (*EAF*)

problems, the MiG-19s continued to fly patrols. Their CO, Alaa Barakat, recalled that before the Six Day War, Egyptian pilots used the British tactical 'fluid four' formation, rather than the tighter Soviet 'finger four'.

The precarious peace in the Middle East was shaken in 1964 when clashes increased along the Israeli-Syrian border. On the Israeli-Egyptian frontier, however, United Nations observers in Sinai recorded very few problems, except for frequent cross-border overflights by mostly Israeli aircraft. On 23 July 1963, the IDF/AF used the anniversary of the 1952 Egyptian Revolution to once again demonstrate its ability to overfly Egyptian territory. This resulted in a clash with two MiG-17s – not MiG-19s, as was reported at the time – with the UARAF claiming to have downed at least one Israeli jet. In fact no aircraft were lost on either side.

A line-up of MiG-21F-13s from the UARAF's first squadron, seen on 26 October 1964. The nearest aircraft bears the serial number 5006 (*EAF*)

Just over three years later, on 29 November 1966, the MiG-19s were in combat for the first time. Having probed the border to test Israeli defences, two MiG-19s were intercepted by two Israeli Mirage IIIs. One MiG fell to a MATRA R.530 missile – the first time it had been used in combat – and the other was hit by cannon fire.

Another little-known aspect of the MiG-19's Egyptian service was its use in Yemen, where an Egyptian expeditionary force helped the Republican government against Royalist tribesmen in a bitter civil war. But only a few MiG-19s were sent to this far southern corner of Arabia.

Egypt, or the UAR as it then was, first expressed an interest in the MiG-21 in 1961, and the following year the USSR agreed to supply 40 to oppose the Mirage IIICs which Israel had on order. At this stage the MiG-21 had no all-weather or ground-attack capability, while its dog-fighting limitations reflected the fact that the aircraft was designed to attack large NATO bombers. Furthermore, Warsaw Pact fighters were intended to be used under very close ground control, which was not available in Egypt at that time. Even the MiG-21F-13's cannon was supposed to be a close-range weapon to finish off an already damaged bomber.

The first Egyptian pilots to convert to the MiG-21 were experienced squadron leaders or flight lieutenants, and by 1964 Egypt had about 60 MiG-21F-13s, probably forming two squadrons. Clearly these first units faced problems. For example, Egypt's first MiG-21s were not equipped with a blind landing radio ground control or guidance system. A temporary solution was found in the installation of arrestor-nets halfway down the runways. Soviet training was also highly orthodox.

An Egyptian pilot completes his preflight checks in a MiG-21F-13 in 1965. Note that the serial number, 5172, has been applied with stencils. This seems to have been characteristic of some of the early MiG-21s supplied to Egypt, and might indicate application prior to delivery from the USSR (*EAF*)

An unnamed Egyptian MiG-21F-13 pilot stares off into the middle distance for the benefit of the camera in 1964 (*EAF*)

Three of Egypt's first MiG-21 pilots, photographed in 1964. The man in the middle is believed to be Fuad Kamal, who commanded a recreated 'big squadron' of surviving MiG-21s after the initial Israeli assault on 5 June 1967 (*EAF*)

MiG-21F-13 squadron CO Sami Marei dismounts from his aircraft at an unnamed airfield during an inspection by Egyptian Minister of Defence Marshal Hakim Amer on 20 May 1967. Marei survived the Six Day War and shot down an Israeli aircraft in combat on 3 November 1968, but was himself shot down and killed on 26 February the following year (*EAF*)

Egypt received its first 45 to 50 MiG-21FLs in 1965, and reached operational status in 1966. The designation FL was used both for the export version of the MiG-21PFM and for an Indian-built version of the jet. However, the PFM and the Indian (HAL factory) FL had a twin-barrelled Gsh-23 mm cannon in an externally mounted pod beneath the fuselage.

Prior to the Six Day War, Egyptian MiG-21FLs did not have guns, being armed solely with a pair of heat-seeking R-3S 'Atoll' missiles. These jets could more properly be designated MiG-21PFs, and in most respects were was even less suited to the kind of fighting involving Arab pilots than the F-13. The latter at least had reasonably good cockpit visibility and a powerful 30 mm cannon. The MiG-21FLs actually came to be seen as a disaster for the UARAF.

Egyptian air tactics and strategy were largely modelled on Soviet doctrine, with interceptions relying on ground-based radars and control to vector pilots to their targets. Such set-piece tactics, when combined with the limited flying experience of many pilots, clearly reduced their effectiveness in traditional manoeuvring combat or dogfights. At squadron level, however, the men were confident. Kadri el-Hamid commented on Egypt's MiG-21 operations before the Six Day War;

'We used to fly over Israel and do reconnaissance at a height of 18 km (11 miles). They shot at us with their Hawk missiles, but because of our height they didn't hit us. We were flying over Israeli territory, and we stayed over it just a short time so the Mirages couldn't catch us either. None of us thought we would fight with Israel, but we felt that we were very good.'

SYRIA AND IRAQ

About 35 to 40 MiG-19Ss were obtained by the Syrian Air Force (SyAAF), probably after the break-up of the union with Egypt. In 1961, it started receiving 36 MiG-21F-13s with which it planned to form a single air brigade of three squadrons, the 8th, 10th and 11th. The first unit was reportedly operational by 1962, but very little is known about the early Syrian service of the MiG-19 and MiG-21. Pilot training was relatively slow, and there were considerable equipment problems. About 45 MiG-21F-13s had eventually been delivered by 1966, and that same year the Israeli spy Eliyahu Cohen's interest in them cost him his life. From 1966, the SyAAF also obtained around 15 MiG-21FLs – enough for one squadron – and six to eight MiG-21U conversion trainers.

The MiG-19S was introduced into Iraqi Air Force (IrAF) service from 1961. A further 50 MiG-19s were subsequently delivered, but it was probably the first batch which was reportedly handed over to the Egyptians in the summer of 1965, since the latter described these as 'second-hand' aircraft. Around 60 MiG-21F-13s were delivered to Iraq between 1963-1966, and in 1965 Algeria also received its first MiG-21F-13s.

Syrian Air Force MiG-19Ss are seen from the control tower on an unnamed airfield prior to the Six Day War (*Tom Cooper collection*)

The first IrAF unit to receive the MiG-21F-13 was the 17th Sqn, formed in 1962, which along with the 1st Fighter-Reconnaissance Squadron were the Iraqis' élite interceptor units for the next 30 years. In fact the 17th Sqn was also the first to fly the MiG-21MF and subsequently the MiG-25.

The first Iraqi unit to fly MiG-19s was the 11th Sqn, which received 12 aircraft in 1962. The IrAF was training very intensively at this time, with pilots flying 20-22 hours per month, and conducting live-firing exercises every Sunday (two jets crashed during early training). Air-to-ground sorties were typically flown, and pilots received very little aerial gunnery instruction.

As in Syria, crew training was constantly interrupted by political unrest within the armed forces. The IrAF was hit especially hard by purges, losing almost half its pilots. In February 1963 IrAF Hunters and MiG-21s from Habbaniyah air base bombed the defence ministry building in Baghdad until the dictator, Brig Gen Abdul Karim Qassem, surrendered. However, the IrAF was on the losing side in the next coup attempt in 1965, and even more personnel were purged.

Above and left
This Iraqi Air Force MiG-21F-13, serial number 534, was flown to Israel by Iraqi defector Capt Monir Radfa of the 17th Sqn on 12 August 1966. He also brought manuals with him, thus giving Israel the technical secrets of a brand new interceptor which formed the main fighting force of emerging Arab air power (*Tom Cooper collection*)

On 16 August 1966, IrAF Capt Monir Radfa of the 11th Sqn took off on a routine training mission, but flew his MiG-21F-13 over Jordan to Israel. Radfa's action was planned by Mossad, the Israeli secret service, which had found this Orthodox Christian pilot unhappy with the way he was treated in the IrAF. The affair threw a dark shadow over the air force, especially when some weeks later three more Iraqi pilots defected with their MiG-21s to Jordan. All of these men were duly granted political asylum, but their aircraft were hastily returned to Iraq.

An Egyptian military delegation is introduced to the CO of an Iraqi Air Force MiG-21F-13 squadron – probably the 17th – in early 1967. The Egyptian delegation included Mustafa Shalabi el-Hinnawy, and was part of an effort to coordinate Arab air strength more effectively (*El-Hinnawy*)

Once things settled down, Iraq ordered 60 more MiG-21PFs and a few MiG-21US conversion trainers in 1966. They were intended to equip four squadrons, but by the spring of 1967 the IrAF still only had two operational MiG-21 units. When not being affected by unrest in Baghdad, Iraqi MiG-21 and MiG-19 squadrons were involved in combat operations against Kurdish rebels in northern and eastern Iraq throughout 1966. Initial Iraqi experience with MiG-21s was not, however, particularly positive. The main problems were similar to those faced by other Arab air forces. When the MiG-21 was exported, the whole support system was rarely purchased – if it was available, it was supplied for the defence of small areas only. Countries like Egypt and Iraq are huge, and the MiGs frequently operated far beyond the zones covered by ground-control-intercept (GCI) stations.

Additional problems were recalled by Maj Samir, an Iraqi MiG-21PF pilot exiled since the late 1960s;

'The R-13 (R-2L "Spin Scan") radar was not operational at speeds over Mach 1.2 because of the cooling system, which took the form of a narrow annular slot girdling the cone directly behind the radome. Relying on air flow through the intake, this system effectively ceased functioning at speeds above Mach 1.2 as the cone slid forward to reduce the air flow, with the result that the radar would either overheat or had to be turned off. Pilots hated the R-13, so they rarely used it actively. It was far better to trust the best detection system around – "Mark 1 eyeball".'

THE UNEXPECTED ASSAULT

The Six Day War came as a complete surprise to UARAF pilots, if not to their leaders. In April 1967, an exchange of artillery fire between Israel and Syria escalated into a full-scale tank and air battle, with six Syrian MiG-21s fighters being downed, while the IDF/AF claimed to have suffered no losses. This caused such shock in Egypt that the UARAF's commander, Mahmud Sidki, summoned a meeting of high-ranking air force officers at Abu Suweir. He announced that he was going to Syria with Field Marshal Fawzy to tell the Syrians to cool the situation because Egypt would not be ready to take on Israel until 1972. On 15 May Nasser announced that Egypt would not attack unless it was itself attacked.

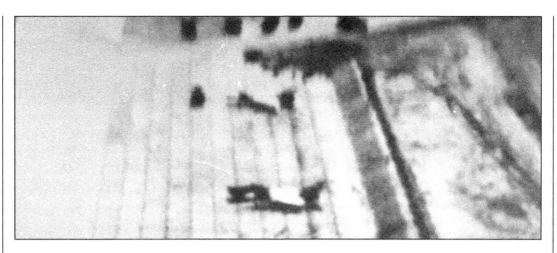

A blurred Israeli gun-camera still of Egyptian UARAF MiG-21s in their revetments on 5 June 1967. These World War 2-style protections at an unnamed air base offered no defence against the type of attack launched by the Israelis (*IDF*)

The UARAF had been placed on alert 24 four hours earlier, and on the 22nd Nasser took the opportunity of a highly-publicised conference at an air base to say he had evidence of an imminent Israeli threat to Syria. Despite continuing diplomatic efforts to lesson tensions, Israel and its Arab neighbours mobilised for war.

At this point the UARAF was portrayed as a formidable force, posing a mortal threat to Israel. The reality, though, was different. Its fighter strength numbered 144 MiG-21s and 40 MiG-19s. Average MiG-21 operational readiness rates varied from 60 to 65 per cent, while the special problems associated with the MiG-19s sometimes lowered their rates even further. Most air bases were concentrated along the Suez Canal, around Cairo and in the Nile Delta, but only a few could accommodate modern combat jets. The result was severe overcrowding. Fuad Kamal, who commanded a MiG-21 air regiment, recalled the stresses of this period;

'My HQ was at Abu Suweir during the June War. We didn't have anywhere near enough shelters for our aircraft, particularly as there were so many aircraft on the base. There were two MiG-21 squadrons and an Su-7 squadron. Just before the June War, an Il-28 (jet bomber) unit was also brought into Abu Suweir. The place was very full of aircraft. In fact it was a crowded mess. We didn't even have enough accommodation for our personnel, as well as enough offices for squadron briefings and so on.'

Moving squadrons also caused considerable confusion. For example, 12 MiG-21s and eight MiG-19s, with 18 pilots, went to Milayz, while a MiG-19 unit moved back and forth between Milayz and Hurghada, responding to a successful Israeli attempt to lure fighters from Sinai.

On the eve of the Six Day War, the UARAF had approximately 20,000 men, but was acutely short of combat pilots, for only 125 were capable of flying modern fighting jets. However, morale among Egyptian pilots was high, especially for those who had combat experience in Yemen. Like many other pilots, Ahmed Atef felt confident before the Six Day War;

'Everyone believed we were the biggest fighting force in the Middle East, which was the propaganda at the time, and that we could even threaten the American Sixth Fleet. Everyone thought that if there was a war with Israeli it would only last 24 hours and would be a walkover to Tel Aviv.'

While Israeli aircraft flew over Sinai to test UARAF reaction times, Egyptian MiG-21s made high altitude flights over Israel. A few low-level

Said Othman was one of the youngest UARAF MiG-21 pilots at el-Milayz, in the Sinai peninsula. He managed to take off while the Israelis were attacking the base, taking on the enemy single-handedly, but was soon shot down and killed (*EAF*)

These MiG-21s of Fuad Kamal's No 5 Air Regiment were photographed by an Israeli jet during a post-strike reconnaissance mission flown shortly after the first air strikes of 5 June 1967. The MiG-21FL at the bottom of the frame appears to be undamaged – several aircraft survived, or could be repaired, to start Egypt's fight-back the following day (*IDF*)

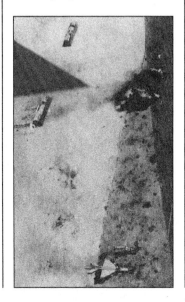

MiG-21 sorties ventured over the southern Israeli air bases, but a longer flight by Fuad Kamal was more ambitious, as he recalled;

'One evening I was out on the tarmac at Abu Suweir and two Israeli jets flew over us very low at dusk. They were too low for our radar to pick up. My pilots were furious, and couldn't understand how such a thing could happen. I said it was easy, and to prove it I decided to do the same. I took off, crossed the frontier and flew north-north-east. I flew a circuit, going right over their flying school and saw training aircraft in the pattern. I could see people pointing at me. I went as far as Haifa, where the fuel light started to flicker, so I turned towards the coast then turned again, flying very low along the beach, filming anything interesting along the way.'

By 2 June Nasser realised that Israel would attack, but the only precautions taken were to bring some aircraft back from exposed forward bases in Sinai to supposed safety west of the Suez Canal. The question of why no MiG-21s were in the air at the time of the Israeli assault has never been adequately answered. Egyptian MiGs had been flying standing patrols throughout daylight hours, but these were ended on the evening of 3 June. Instead, there were only the dawn patrols.

The Israeli surprise attack on 5 June struck ten Egyptian airfields. The first wave of 160 Israeli jets took off at 0800 hrs Egyptian time, and subsequent ones followed at ten-minute intervals over the next 90 minutes. The IDF/AF's first targets were Egypt's MiG-21 bases. Israeli aircraft entered Egyptian airspace at extremely low altitude, and technicians manning Egyptian radar systems saw nothing. As a result, the UARAF's interceptor bases were caught entirely by surprise.

That much is well known. Far less publicised were the desperate attempts of pilots and ground crews to resist. El-Milayz was the UARAF's most advanced interceptor base, and it was from there that Kadri el-Hamid calmly watched the Israeli aircraft approaching. He recalled;

'I was in the tower by the radar, and saw the whole scene. I heard the sound of many aircraft. I said to myself, "The MiG-19s from Hurghada are flying to el-Milayz and back". I thought, "Not those MiG-19s again. They are a terrible nuisance". I saw the bombs falling from four Ouragans, two from each.'

The Israelis did face resistance, however. Said Othman was one of his squadron's newest pilots, and his groundcrew recalled what happened;

'Lt Said Othman jumped in his MiG-21 and shouted to the technicians, "Get this 'plane moving!" His voice competed with the sound of bombs, but they heard him and obeyed, and so he took off. He started to attack the Israeli formations but they shot him down and he was killed.'

Since Kadri el-Hamid and the other pilots had no aircraft left to fly, they took a lorry and drove through the Mitla Pass to Cairo. Back at UARAF HQ, their commander was told to select his eight best pilots and to fly to Iraq in a civilian airliner. They expected to be able to bring some MiG-21s back with them, but the Iraqis refused.

The disaster at Abu Suweir was just as bad, as Fuad Kamal, an air brigadier at the base, recalled;

'The first I knew about the attack was a loud explosion. It was the runway being bombed. Seconds later two Israeli aircraft came over very low and there were more explosions. They had dropped their "dibber" (runway-piercing) bombs on the runway intersections. I jumped into a jeep and drove fast to the ops room, which was quite a long way away. I telephoned my squadron leader in Sinai (at el-Milayz) and told him to scramble his aircraft to cover Abu Suweir. But he told me that exactly the same had happened where he was. So I called Inshas, and they said the same. Two of the ready aircraft did take off on a sub-runway. One was shot down while retracting its undercarriage (the pilot was killed). The other then flew cover, before safely landing on a sub-runway.'

Awad Hamdi survived a similar sortie at Abu Suweir;

'We scrambled after the first attacks without orders. The Israelis had bombed the runway intersections. I figured that by flying an aircraft without any drop tanks I could get into the air. Our base commander marked where I left the ground. I cleared the holes by only six to eight metres. A short time later I spotted the Israelis and made a rendezvous with a group of four aircraft. My wingman fired an "Atoll" at an Israeli jet, but we were at low altitude and it just flew into the ground. The MiG-21FL that I was flying had no cannon, just two "Atolls". I aimed at the centre-point of the exhaust of a Mystere and launched my missile. It hit close to the Mystere and then I engaged again.'

Fuad Kamal continued;

'Between Israeli attacks, the ground personnel pulled surviving aircraft, including some damaged ones, out of the exposed area. They put them under trees outside the airfield and in other sheltered areas. Meanwhile, the delayed action bombs continued to go off. After sunset the maintenance crews started to assemble aircraft during the night, combining undamaged parts from damaged aircraft – wings, tail units and so on.'

Not far away, at Fayid air base, a government delegation had been due to arrive at 0900 hrs, but their aircraft could not land until 0910 hrs because of fog. Tahsin Zaki, the CO of a mixed Su-7 and MiG-21 air regiment, recalled;

'We were completely surprised, standing beside our jets for that morning's training sortie. We saw two Super Mystere B2s flying very low across the airfield from west to east, releasing their bombs on the main runway, while other aircraft attacked the MiG-21s on standby with rockets and gunfire. Some Egyptian pilots tried to take off with their fighters but could not because the main runway was holed. So they started taxiing to try to take-off from the sub-runway, only to find that it was blocked by the minister's aircraft that had landed a few minutes earlier and was then hit where it had stopped.'

The isolated Egyptian airfield at Hurghada, on the Red Sea, was not on the Israelis' first strike target list, and its MiG-19s flew combat air patrols before the IDF/AF attacked in the early afternoon. Abd al-Moneim el-Tawil had landed by the time the Israelis arrived after 1300 hrs. A flight of MiG-19s and another of MiG-21s that were also in the air were called back to defend the base, but by the time they arrived the Israelis were leaving and there was no combat. Most remaining MiG-19s were then flown to Cairo International, from where they operated until the end of the war.

Alaa Barakat explained what happened next;

'Only four MiG-19 pilots remained in Hurghada. No 1, Sqn Ldr Shalash, No 2, Capt Mustafa Darwish, No 3, Capt Fatih Selim, No 4, 1Lt Abdul Rahman Sidki. They stopped Israeli paratroopers seizing

1Lt Abdel Moneim Mursi also managed to take off from a short length of untouched runway at Abu Suweir on 5 June 1967, and he subsequently damaged one of the attacking Israeli aircraft, although he was initially credited with shooting down two. Returning to base, Mursi failed to spot a bomb crater while landing into the sun and was killed when his MiG-21 exploded (*EAF*)

Sharm el-Shaykh (it fell later). They were patrolling the area when Shalash and Darwish engaged four Mirages which were escorting three Noratlas transports. Selim and Sidki then saw another flight of Mirages. Selim ordered, "Drop auxiliary tanks", and went after the Noratlases – they claimed to have shot down two. Meanwhile, Shalash and Darwish were in a dogfight with Mirages and were shot down.'

Other sources indicate that only one Noratlas was destroyed.

Inshas was was one of the UARAF's most important MiG-21 bases, and it was duly one of the first to be attacked. Given the confusion, it is not surprising that there are conflicting accounts of the death of the resident brigade's CO, Sami Fuad. One version states that he engaged four aircraft, damaging one, before himself being shot down by an Egyptian Air Defence missile. The only victory which can be confirmed was that of Nabil Shoukry. Two hours after the first strike three MiG-21FLs and one MiG-21F-13 took off. Shoukry described what then happened;

'I did a CAP over Bilbays. Then the base called me again and said there were Mirages over Inshas. So I flew over and saw two Mirages to the left. I closed up behind them until I saw the wingman's helmet. I could only look, as the limitations of my "Atoll" missile prevented me from shooting at him. They dived down and ran, and so I got a chance. I followed them and fired an "Atoll" at the leader. The first missile hit, and there was heavy smoke. I looked for the wingman but didn't see him, so I decided to launch a second missile at the aircraft. The Mirage exploded and pitched up in a stall turn, and then the nose went right down.'

At Abu Suweir, Fuad Kamal was angered by some of the orders he was receiving. He recalled;

'Some orders from HQ were so stupid that I simply didn't carry them out. In fact I was rude to some of the senior officers, and when one of them gave us a particularly stupid order I told him, "You come and do it!" One example of an impossible or stupid order was "Take four aircraft and attack Israel"! I simply ignored it.'

The Egyptian Air Force claims to have shot down no more than four enemy aircraft in air combat on the first day. Seven of the 27 Egyptian fighter pilots who became airborne made contact with the enemy, but 17 lost their lives – mostly before their wheels left the ground. Unofficial Egyptian sources claim that the UARAF made about 60 sorties, including ground-attack missions and flying aircraft to safety. The Israelis at first claimed to have shot down 26 Egyptian aircraft, but the official Israeli air combat claim for 5 June now stands at six MiG-21s, five MiG-19s, one MiG-17 and an Il-14, which actually made a successful forced landing near Fayid.

Between 20 and 30 Egyptian combat aircraft survived intact at the end of the war's first day, excluding

Sami Fuad was 9th Air Brigade CO at Inshas, which was home to a significant number of MiG-21s. He managed to take off and engage the enemy during the Israeli assault of 5 June 1967 and was credited with damaging an aircraft before being shot down in error by an Egyptian air defence missile (*EAF*)

This low-level reconnaissance photograph was taken at Cairo West or Abu Suweir by an Israeli Mirage IIIC soon after the first wave of air attacks on 5 June 1967. Boasting a damaged fin leading edge, this MiG-21FL was in the process of being armed with UB-16 57 mm rocket launchers when it was strafed (*IDF via Tom Cooper*)

Lt Hasan el-Qusri was another MiG-21FL pilot who got airborne from Inshas during the Israeli attacks of 5 June 1967. He was initially credited with shooting down an Israeli aircraft before running out of fuel and baling out near the coast. El-Qusri returned to Inshas by road, and almost immediately took off on another mission, during which he was credited with destroying a second Israeli jet over the Sinai desert. Having once again run his fuel tanks dry, he attempted to make an emergency landing on a road but his aircraft flipped over and el-Qusri was killed. It now appears that his victory claims were optimistic (*EAF*)

those based in Yemen. Others had been lightly damaged, and through the following night Egyptian technicians worked to make as many operational as possible. Once the scale of the disaster became apparent, Nasser telephoned Algeria's President Hoari Boumedienne that afternoon to explain that the UARAF had lost few pilots. Boumedienne then decided to send as many aircraft as the Algerian Air Force (QJA) could spare. These included a 'big' squadron of MiG-21F-13s, forming part of an air brigade commanded by Abdelrezak Bouhara.

Not surprisingly, Egyptian pilots were furious at what had happened. But the start of the second day (6 June) saw Egypt's surviving MiG fighters scattered around various air bases. Fuad Kamal recalled;

'At Abu Suweir, our four surviving MiG-21s took off at first light from a sub-runway. One was shot down by one of our own Surface-to-Air Missiles (SAMs). The missile caused an automatic ejection. I saw it, and there were flames coming from the seat, but still the parachute opened. The pilot had serious burns and was sent to England for hospital treatment.'

Fuad Kamal's deputy, Faruk el-Ghazzawi, also flew two sorties that day;

'I flew two air-to-ground missions with 57 mm rocket-pods against Israeli targets near the Mitla Pass. It was hit and run, because we were a very small number of aircraft and we didn't have time to evaluate what damage we caused.'

But with so few aircraft there was little the men at Abu Suweir could do, and so they were sent to Cairo West with Fuad Kamal. He said;

'By then eight or ten more of our aircraft were repaired. Surviving MiG-21s from other bases also arrived, and they were concentrated at Cairo West. From this a new wing or "big squadron" was formed. We had enough aircraft for two squadrons, and I was put in command of this new unit.'

By dawn on the 6th, UARAF mechanics had made six MiG-19s serviceable in a hanger at Fayid. At first light Alaa Barakat led a mission by four of them to protect Egyptian Army units in Sinai, but no enemy aircraft were seen. Barakat continued;

'At noon on 6 June a flight of four MiG-19s, led by Sqn Ldr Taysir Hashish, engaged six Mirages over the Bitter Lakes and fought for 12 minutes. During this combat the No 3, named Idris, did a split but was shot down. His No 2 (the No 4 of the flight), Salah Danish, was also shot down and baled out. He landed near the coal mines in Sinai. The miners were already preparing to evacuate the area, but Danish complained that he had hurt his back during the ejection and needed to rest a while. As a result he was captured by the Israelis, and was thereafter nicknamed "the lazy pilot".

'Another MiG-19 section, comprising Hishmat Sidki and Saad Zaghloul, was intercepted by eight Mirages and both were shot down. Hishmat Sidki ejected near the Canal and was unhurt. Zaghloul landed deeper in Sinai and teamed up with some retreating Egyptian soldiers. They walked for a long way and, without water, Zaghloul had to drink his own urine. They were then captured by Israeli soldiers near the Canal. One of the Israelis opened fire on the soldiers, but his machine-gun ran out of bullets before reaching Zaghloul, so they let him go. The soldiers were killed.'

These Algerian MiG-21F-13s were photographed in the 1960s. The Algerian Air Force sent sizeable contingents of MiG-17s and MiG-21s to Egypt during the June 1967 War, although the MiG-21s do not seem to have entered service until immediately after the cease-fire. They then played a significant role in the early stages of Egypt's fight-back (*Tom Cooper collection*)

Egyptian pilots arrived in Algeria to collect QJA MiGs. Although Algerian MiG-17s returned to Egypt in time to take part in the fighting, the MiG-21s apparently arrived shortly after war had ended. But UARAF resistance was stiffening, and the IDF/AF lost 15 aircraft on day two, including two shot down by Egyptian aircraft. In return, the Israelis claimed to have shot down 19 Egyptian aircraft, although this was later reduced to a MiG-19, a MiG-21 and two Su-7s!

For the UARAF, the war's third and fourth days focussed on dispersing vulnerable surviving aircraft while rebuilding a small fighting force of MiG-21s at Cairo West and Inshas. Four MiG-19s led by Alaa Barakat attacked Israeli tanks near Bir el-Abid on 7 June and suffered no losses. At first the Israelis claimed that three of these aircraft had been shot down, although this was subsequently reduced to one MiG-19. Later that day, Barakat's aircraft were ordered to withdraw to Cairo International to join MiG-19s already there. The IDF/AF admitted losing two jets in air combat on 7 June, but claimed to have downed one MiG-21, one MiG-19 and four other aircraft.

Abd el-Moneim el-Tawil flew a MiG-19 mission on the 8th against Israeli tanks advancing towards the Suez Canal. He recalled;

'We were jumped by a standing patrol of eight to twelve Mirages. One MiG-19 was shot down and one was damaged, but it stayed with us. We defended ourselves successfully and then flew home. On the way back the pilot of the damaged aircraft baled out okay before we reached Cairo International.'

At first the Egyptian authorities stated the MiG-19s had shot down one Mirage, but this claim was later abandoned.

On the fourth day there was a sudden increase in Egyptian air activity, largely in support of the Army as it attempted to retreat from Sinai. At Cairo West, Fuad Kamal recalled;

'Starting from 8 June, the new "wing" was given a new number, as were its two new squadrons. Their pilots came from all over, including Inshas. When we started flying again there was a new mood. Our function was interception and "free hunting" as far as the Suez Canal, where the Israelis were still attacking our airfields. We weren't given the task of covering our ground-attack aircraft.'

There was a similar mood at Inshas, whose MiG-21 pilots were still involved in ground-attack missions east of the Canal. Nabil Shoukry flew his second sortie of the day with, as he put it, 'two pods of those awful (ground-attack) rockets, and we attacked some tanks in the north Sinai.

'After we passed the Canal, we saw two Mirages coming from the left. So I put the afterburner on, jettisoned the belly tank and saw that the Mirages were going to attack. I told my leader, "There's a Mirage behind you". He reversed. At that moment his MiG-21 exploded after being hit by cannon fire. After that the Mirage headed towards el-Arish. I put the nose down with maximum afterburner, but I had those two rocket-pods which created a lot of drag. I levelled off with the Mirage within a mile, but had no way to close because he was accelerating. I started firing unguided rockets from each pod at him but I didn't succeed.'

By 9 June it was clear that Egypt had lost. But there was no cease-fire yet. Egyptian claims for this day have not been made public, but the IDF/AF claimed one MiG-19 and four other aircraft. President Nasser publicly accepted responsibility for the disaster and resigned – for a few hours at least.

Available evidence indicates that the UARAF flew about 133 missions with surviving or repaired aircraft during the Six Day War. When it was over, Egypt admitted having lost almost 65 per cent of its strength either on the ground or in the air – 250 fighters and fighter-bombers and 55 bombers, plus an unspecified number of support aircraft. The Israelis initially claimed to have destroyed 451 on the ground and between 50 and 60 in the air – including about 100 MiG-21s and 29 MiG-19s – during 64 air combats. This was a huge exaggeration. Nasser also admitted that 34 Egyptian pilots and six aircrew had been killed, with a number of others wounded.

Initial Egyptian claims were even more inflated, but were later reduced to 72 Israeli aircraft destroyed. The IDF/AF admitted 45 losses on all fronts, while outside observers put the figure between 55 and 60. Years later, unofficial Israelis sources admitted ten IDF/AF aircraft downed in air combat on all fronts. Independent sources put this figure at 11, plus another resulting from fuel exhaustion. In fact several Israeli aircraft reportedly downed by ground fire probably fell to Egyptian fighters.

SYRIA UNREADY

While the Syrians were trained almost exclusively by Soviet and Egyptian instructors, Iraqi training was undertaken with the help of Indian and British personnel. Like their Indian counterparts in Egypt and Egyptian counterparts in Syria, they had problems preparing their students for serious operations. Furthermore, the training received by new Arab MiG-21 pilots in the USSR was largely limited to basic flying. The Soviets would not train their Arab customers in navigation, flying at low-level or in the use of MiGs in manoeuvring combat, especially at low-level.

Nabil Shoukry was one of the few Egyptian MiG-21 pilots to actually shoot down an enemy aircraft on 5 June 1967. Pictured here much later in his career, he was based at Inshas and flying a MiG-21FL when he downed the Mirage IIIC of Capt Yair Nueman of the IDF/AF's élite No 101 Sqn (*EAF*)

An American tourist poses beside the tail and drop-tank of an Egyptian MiG-21FL some months after it was shot down in northern Sinai during the Six Day War
(*R Goldman*)

Serviceability was also poor initially. When the June war broke out, the SyAAF had less than 20 fully operational MiG-21s, while the IrAF had fewer than 20 pilots qualified to fly them in combat.

For the SyAAF, the war began with a strike by 12 MiG-17s, escorted by several MiG-19s and MiG-21s, against the Haifa oil refinery at around 1100 hrs on 5 June. The target was hit, and although the Israelis denied this Arab success as usual, damage was indeed limited because the bombs dropped were small and several failed to explode. Two MiG-17s were downed by ground fire.

Meanwhile, several MiG-17s, MiG-19s and MiG-21s flew CAPs over Damascus. Most had landed to refuel when the Israelis attacked Syrian airfields at around 1400 hrs. The first four Super Mystere B2s surprised the defences and bombed the runways at Dumayr, but then a SyAAF MiG-19 flown by Capt Ghazy al-Wazwazy from the 77th Sqn shot down Capt Dan Sigiri. The Israelis claimed that Sigiri was hit by anti-aircraft fire, ejected and was murdered by civilians.

Five minutes later four Vautours repeated the attack but encountered alerted air defences, resulting in Capt Avraham Weiland being shot down and taken prisoner. The rest of his formation was intercepted by two 5th Sqn MiG-21PFs, one of which was flown by Lt Adeeb al-Gar, who fired both his R-3 'Atoll' missiles in quick succession to increase the probability of a hit. Although al-Gar claimed one aircraft shot down, the Vautours evaded both missiles and escaped southwards.

The large Syrian airfield at al-Mezze, outside Damascus, was simultaneously attacked by four Mystere IVAs, but by flying over Lebanon and around Mount Hermon, this Israeli formation lost the element of surprise and was intercepted by a pair of MiG-17s. The Israeli No 4 was hit by Lt Zuhair al-Baowab's cannon fire and the pilot subsequently ejected over Lebanon. Al-Baowab went on to fly MiG-21s during the War of Attrition. Some ten minutes later, over Tsaikal air base, two new MiG-21PFs engaged four Super Mysteres, but both were shot down. Thanks to the delivery of an Iraqi MiG-21F-13 to Israel in 1966, IDF/AF pilots knew how to outmanoeuvre the MiG. Seasoned SyAAF veteran, Col (ret) 'M' explained;

'During this combat we learned – the wrong way – that, especially at low-level, the engagement envelope of the R-3 "Atoll" missile was so poor that our chances against hard-manoeuvring Israelis were minimal.'

At Homs air base the SyAAF suffered a catastrophe. Eyewitnesses watched in awe as Israeli aircraft attacked the runway. Like other Syrian airfields, the base had at least ten very realistic wooden dummy MiG-17s and MiG-21s. But the Israeli pilots seem to have been well informed about the decoys, and after the attack was over Homs personnel realised that only the real MiGs had been hit. Not a single decoy was destroyed, leading to wild rumours about traitors within SyAAF ranks. Much the same happened at Tsaikal and Marj Ruhayyil.

For the SyAAF, the Six Day War was over almost before it began, and on 5 June the IDF/AF claimed the destruction of 30 of Syria's 36 MiG-21s, including two shot down in air combat. The remaining six jets were flown to airfields in the far north of the country, along with the surviving MiG-17s. For the rest of the war, the SyAAF undertook only a small number of patrols, trying instead to conserve its remaining air power. Consequently, Syrian troops on the Golan Heights were heavily attacked by the IDF/AF and their valiant defence proved vain.

IRAQ HOLDS OUT

The war also came as a surprise to the Iraqis. They had planned to send some squadrons to Syria if war broke out, but when the Israelis attacked Iraqi preparations were incomplete. With the SyAAF being battered and its airfields extensively damaged, this plan was abandoned, although IrAF Hunters flew combat sorties against targets inside Israel. They fought two combats with Israeli Mirages on the morning of the 5th, although the swift crushing of the Egyptian, Jordanian and Syrian air forces subsequently changed the situation before the IrAF could find out what was happening.

At noon on the 5th, four Vautour bombers struck the first blow against Iraq, hitting the H-3/al-Walid air base before the patrolling MiG-21s could react. Despite some communications problems, the Israelis claimed six MiG-21s and six other aircraft destroyed on the ground. All remaining operational Iraqi aircraft were then ordered back to Habbaniyah, in central Iraq. Before this could be done, the IDF/AF launched a second attack against H-3. The Israeli formation appeared over the base as two MiG-21s were taking-off to relieve two Hunters on standing patrol. The result was a short but fierce dogfight which reduced the Israeli strike to a confused series of individual efforts. The results were minimal. They missed several Tu-16s, damaged one Hunter and downed two of the defending MiG-21s.

After this fiasco, the IrAF High Command decided not to even refuel aircraft at H-3, and all patrols were to be flown from Habbaniyah. Because of their short range, Iraqi MiG-21s were now effectively out of the battle, responsibility for the defence of H-3 falling to IrAF Hunters. They shot down a Mirage and a Vautour during the third Israeli air strike on 7 June. The surviving, but now scattered, Mirages and Vautours were then intercepted on their way home by a pair of Syrian MiG-21PFs. The Israelis were flying a straight course at high altitude, which should have made it easier for the MiG pilots to use their R-3s. But, despite being fired from ideal positions, three of the four 'Atolls' missed, while the fourth exploded near a Mirage IIIC and damaged it, but not enough to prevent its pilot landing safely in Israel.

During the evening of the 8th, the Israelis made several attempts to recover crews shot down over H-3. They even despatched a single Noratlas transport, but this was intercepted by a Syrian MiG-21PF. However, both R-3 'Atoll' missiles fired by an unnamed Syrian pilot again lost their lock and missed. That marked the end of Israeli strikes against H-3, as well as the participation of Syrian and Iraqi MiG-19s and MiG-21s in the Six Day War.

The Egyptian and Syrian MiG-21 pilots who clashed with the Israelis before and during the Six Day War were literally 'caught with their trousers down'. Even Israeli Ouragans were outmanoeuvring and shooting down MiG-21s. But bearing in mind that Egyptian and Syrian pilots were not trained for dogfighting, they performed quite well in air combat. Nevertheless, with every Arab pilot killed or removed for political reasons, the Arab air forces lost valuable continuation and experience.

FIGHTING BACK

The period between the end of the Six Day War and the October 1973 War (known to the Israelis as the Yom Kippur War) was especially difficult for Egypt. Yet it was also an heroic one, as the air force fought back from a position of defeat and humiliation.

On 11 June 1967, two days after announcing – and then withdrawing – his resignation, President Nasser fired most of Egypt's senior military officers and his civilian advisers. Many were promptly arrested and sent to prison to await trial. Mahmud Sidki was replaced as air force CO by Gen Madkhur Abu el-Izz, who had commanded the UARAF's Academy at Bilbays. However, Nasser's old revolutionary colleague Field Marshal Hakim Amr refused to accept the blame for Egypt's defeat and was suspected of preparing a show of force to bolster his position. Whatever the truth, Amr's powerplay failed, and he committed suicide. Pro-Nasser and pro-Amr cliques appeared, even in the air force. Several pro-Amr officers were obliged to resign, at least temporarily, while others are believed to have been among those sent to support the Nigerian Federal Air Force during its fight against the breakaway state of Biafra.

Meanwhile, the UARAF began rebuilding itself. Egypt's strategic situation was now far weaker than before the Six Day War, with most of Sinai and all its bases occupied by the Israelis. Several other bases on the western side of the Suez Canal were also too close to the frontline to be used.

About 50 Egyptian combat aircraft had survived the war, to which were added Algerian reinforcements and Soviet re-supplies. In fact the UARAF could have fought on, but the Egyptian Army had been crushed. Fakry el-Gahramy recalled how air force engineers and maintenance crews did an incredible job in reassembling aircraft from undamaged wings, tail units and fuselages. At the same time, camouflage paint schemes were applied to all Egyptian combat aircraft within days of the cease-fire. Since no aircraft paint was available, air force headquarters purchased large quantities of car paint! Most aircraft at Nile Delta air bases were painted 'sand and spinach', while those on desert bases were usually finished in 'sand and stone'.

It took time to return wounded pilots to duty, and consequently considerable burdens were placed upon those available, resulting in physical exhaustion, nervous breakdowns, blood-clots and other symptoms. The best and most experienced had been selected for the new 'big squadron' of MiG-21s commanded by Fuad Kamal at Cairo West. This subsequently became the élite No 47 Sqn. Among those selected for it was Kadri el-Hamid, who become a nightfighter pilot. Fuad remained in command for two months before requesting a transfer.

Within a week of the cease-fire a few MiG-21s were sent on reconnaissance missions over newly-established Israeli positions in Sinai. Many MiG-19 pilots now transferred to MiG-17s, at least during this tense period, while the surviving MiG-19s were held back for internal defence. No replacement MiG-19s were obtained from the Soviet bloc, and the existing MiG-19 air brigade was disbanded.

The wreckage of this Egyptian UARAF MiG-21 was found in the Suez Canal after being supposedly shot down by Israeli fighters in June 1967. As the aircraft was clearly camouflaged, the combat must have taken place soon after the cease-fire, possibly in July 1967 (*IDF via Tom Cooper*)

Meanwhile, the USSR replaced Egypt's lost military equipment in a massive airlift lasting about 40 days. An-12 transports, each carrying a fighter or fighter-bomber, unloaded directly at operational airfields. Warsaw Pact military advisers were installed at virtually every level in Egypt's armed services. Egypt also had the MiG-21s sent by Algeria. The most important tasks were to restore radar coverage and develop low altitude combat techniques. As Fuad Kamal explained, the Air Defence HQ could not even see its own reconnaissance aircraft, let alone those of the enemy. The Egyptians also dispersed their aircraft at minor airfields and road strips, while the task of developing effective aircraft shelters was another urgent priority.

On 1 July the Egyptian Army halted an Israeli attempt to push northwards along the Suez Canal causeway towards Port Fuad, but Egypt's MiG-21 pilots were refused permission to cross the waterway. A few did so nevertheless, and on the 4th a MiG-17 was shot down over the Gulf of Suez. Israel claimed two more on the 7th. The following day, the first air combat between Egyptian and Israeli fighters saw four MiG-21s fight two Mirages just east of Qantara. One MiG-21 was damaged or shot down and the Egyptians claimed two Mirages damaged. After this, Egyptian pilots were kept under stricter control.

On 14 July the air force got its turn to hit back, launching a major raid which took the Israelis by surprise. UARAF aircraft flew 256 missions and the enemy pulled their most exposed troops back from the Canal. Farid Harfush, who flew the following day, reported;

'I was stationed at Cairo West. On 15 July 1967 I was on alert and they launched us. I was No 4 of the group. We went east as fast as we could, and we had instructions to join an air engagement between Israeli and Egyptian aeroplanes. I saw two Mirages, and reported them to my leader. We were flying supersonic at this time at an altitude of 7000 m (22,750 ft). We did a "split-S" and got behind the Mirages. After some hard turns, I saw my No 1 fighting with a single Mirage. So I came in and tried to protect him. My No 1 launched a missile and it hit the Israeli jet. The Mirage exploded and I didn't see the pilot bale out. My section did not suffer any losses, but some were shot down from the other flights.'

The Israelis admitted losing a Mirage, but almost inevitably said it had been brought down by a SAM. In return they claimed three MiG-21s, later reduced to two, and three other aircraft. Further clashes occurred on 19 and 20 July, without lost to either side, but to the surprise of Egyptian pilots this counter-attack then ended abruptly.

Most of the injured pilots had by now returned to duty, and others came back from advanced training in the USSR. But Egypt was still short of combat-rated fast jet pilots. Within weeks of the ending of the Six Day War, about 300 cadets began primary training. Many experienced MiG pilots trained newly-arrived members of their squadrons while also carrying out operational duties. Matters were complicated by the presence of different types of MiG-21 within each unit, and pilots often did not know what they would be flying since aircraft were allocated according to availability. And with the Soviet Union rejecting Egypt's request for more modern equipment, Madkhur el-Izz and his men had to work with what they had. Egypt's MiG-21s were not the latest models, but they were available in quantity and they were cheap to buy.

Life at the MiG-21 squadrons remained hectic though the late summer and early autumn of 1967. The air bases were like beehives, with mechanics and arming personnel busy while pilots sat at first stage alert in their cockpits, awaiting the red flare which ordered them to scramble. Other pilots at second stage alert ate, slept and played cards beside their aircraft. Most penetrations of Israeli-occupied Sinai were on a small scale, usually by reconnaissance patrols of two aircraft.

In August, Israeli flak fire claimed an unidentified Egyptian jet, the pilot ejecting safely within Egyptian territory. On 12 September Egyptian anti-aircraft claimed an Israeli Mirage, while the Egyptian Navy seized its chance to hit back by sinking the Israeli flagship on 21 October. Israeli artillery retaliated by shelling Suez, while Israeli aircraft attacked naval facilities in Alexandria and Port Said. Egyptian pilots were not allowed to intervene, and shortly afterwards Madkhur Abu el-Izz resigned. Many in the air force believed he had been removed because he had supported his pilots too vocally when they were criticised by Soviet advisers.

On 3 November el-Izz was replaced by Mustafa Shalabi el-Hinnawy, who had flown Spitfires in 1948. After returning from the Joint Arab Air Command in Jordan, Hinnawy played a senior role in the commission which analysed Egypt's catastrophic defeat. Whereas Izz's task had been to revive the UARAF, Hinnawy supervised a comprehensive reorganisation, with intensive training, new bases and hardened hangers for combat aircraft. This initial reorganisation was apparently based upon, or was perhaps a continuation of, the existing system of code-numbers to identify Egyptian airfields. Rather than indentifying individual squadrons or air brigades, it referred to units flying certain types of aircraft and based at one specific airfield. These sometimes formed a full air brigade, while others consisted of one or more squadrons from an air brigade which was divided between two airfields. The system may also only have been used at Air Defence planning level, since it seems to have been unknown to operational pilots. Action against Israel was largely restricted to reconnaissance sorties, although there were occasional clashes.

Egypt now began receiving newer versions of the MiG-21, but they did not necessarily represent an improvement. The MiG-21PFS had a new engine and additional fuel tanks, which improved manoeuvrability and range, but there was still no cannon, and it remained ineffective as a dog-fighter. However, the UARAF was now making locally-designed modifications and some, perhaps most, of the MiG-21FLs and MiG-21PF were given under-slung pods containing GSh-23 double-barrelled 23 mm cannon, which may have been obtained from India. Ground-attack rocket-pods were also added. Finally, to increase the jet's range, technicians developed larger drop tanks, which were then adopted by the Soviets.

The Egyptians also needed sophisticated aerial reconnaissance cameras, so the British Vinten company supplied long-range oblique photography pods whose dimensions were based on the centreline auxiliary fuel tank of

Mustafa Shalabi el-Hinnawy took command of the Egyptian UARAF early in November 1967. Although his task was primarily to rebuild and re-organise the air force, his pilots also had to fight. El-Hinnawy is seen here decorating one of the top students during a passing out parade at the Egyptian Air Force Academy in 1968. Top students were usually sent to MiG-21 squadrons (*El-Hinnawy*)

a MiG-21. They were used by Egyptian MiG-21s and Su-7s from the start of 1968.

The downgrading of Egypt's remaining MiG-19s to interior defence is considered a mistake by modern Soviet commentators. It might have been more suited to providing close support for subsonic MiG-17 ground-attack jets because it had better dogfighting endurance than the short-winded MiG-21.

Despite occasional clashes, 1968 was a period of preparation for the UARAF, and by the end of that year it is estimated to have had 115 MiG-21s and 80+ MiG-19s combat-ready. If the latter figure is correct, Egypt must have received the MiG-19s reportedly transferred from Syria and Iraq. These formed No 137 Sqn (which is sometimes described as a reserve or operational training unit), or perhaps a nominal air brigade, based at Kafr Daud in 1969. Egypt's fighters were now grouped into an estimated two all-weather and 13 day-fighter squadrons, some of which were new. The six remaining MiGs sent from Algeria in the closing days of the Six Day War returned to the QJA, the rest having been written off.

The Egyptian Air Defence Force (EADF) was established as a separate military service on 1 July 1968. Modelled on the Soviet PVO *Strany*, the EADF had several MiG-21 squadrons assigned to it. They were allocated defence zones, and coordinated their efforts with the anti-aircraft artillery and SAMs, the aircraft being controlled from a United Command Post (UCP) linked to the forward radar network. The greatly enhanced anti-aircraft capabilities of both sides inhibited fighter and ground-attack missions. While Israeli Mirage pilots relied on their powerful gun armament, their Egyptian counterparts flying the MiG-21 had been trained to rely on an automated interception system called *Vozdookh-1*. Although it was more effective in theory than in practice, training on this missile-optimised system deeply influenced Arab pilots. If they chose not to use *Vozdookh-1*, they were reduced to 'hand and eye'.

On 8 September 1968 the Egyptian Army began the offensive phase of Nasser's planned confrontation with Israel with artillery barrages along the Suez Canal. These were supported by aerial reconnaissance missions, while Egypt's MiG-21s were held back to protect returning reconnaissance aircraft. But on 23 October there was a clash above Ismailiya. Egypt claimed three Mirages – Israel denied it. Another massive Egyptian artillery barrage on the 27th was followed by spectacular helicopter-borne Israeli commando raids deep inside Egypt on the 31st.

On 3 November another air combat took place over the northern part of the Suez Canal when four Israeli aircraft crossed the border, only to be intercepted by four MiG-21s. One Mirage was damaged and, unable to keep up with the others, was caught by Egyptian anti-aircraft fire and exploded north of Qantara. This was probably the same combat which involved UARAF MiG-21 pilots Maj Sami Marei, Lt Ibrahim Hamad,

The cockpit of an Egyptian MiG-21PF, as used between 1966 and 1973. Soviet instructors trained their Arab pupils to fight with their heads thrust into the sizeable radar hood and their ears alert for GCI instructions. However, Arab pilots soon learned from bitter experience that they had to become more independent, and manoeuvre their aircraft aggressively, to survive (*Tom Cooper collection*)

Capt Ahmad Nur el-Din and Lt Ahmed Atef, and saw Sami Marei's success verified by Egyptian Army units.

A new air brigade system was introduced in the first half of 1969. Thereafter, the fighter brigades based at Inshas and Mansourah were numbered 102 and 104 respectively, with a third fighter squadron, No 111, being based at Beni Sueif in Upper Egypt. Nos 102 and 104 Brigades provided frontline combat interception, but not all squadrons achieved the same speed of response. Among the best was No 26 which, as an élite unit, had the unofficial nickname of 'The Black Ravens'. Another élite unit was No 25 Sqn, based at Inshas.

The biggest problem for Egypt's MiG-21s was their inability to reach intruders in time, because Israeli aircraft were only over Egyptian territory briefly. Furthermore, radars defending the Egyptian Delta and Cairo were at low altitude, and so had little chance of anticipating such attacks. If standing patrols of MiG-21s were sent into these zones, they themselves became targets for Israeli ambush.

On 3 March Israel claimed that its Mirages had shot down an Egyptian MiG-21. Five days later Nasser announced the start of a war of attrition aimed at destroying Israeli fortifications along the Suez Canal.

At 1235 hrs on the 8th, a flight of MiG-21s on alert was sent against four Mirages flying along the canal from north to south. The Egyptian ground controller sent the MiG pilots on a 90-degree intercept course at an altitude of 6500 ft (200 m). When they sighted the enemy they jettisoned external fuel tanks and attacked. Maj Shamala led the MiG flight, and after a half-roll, he got onto the tail of the closest pair of Mirages. But he then realised that he had dropped his missiles along with his tanks, so he handed the interception over to the second pair. Shamala's error proved fatal, because he got so close that the Mirages spotted him and made an instant combat turn. The second Egyptian pair also made their attack manoeuvre too slowly, being unable to coordinate their fire with the first.

Realising the danger of this situation, the leader of the second pair decided to attack independently, got onto the tail of the rearmost Mirage, launched two missiles and got a hit. Shamala now tried to support his colleague and opened fire, but the turning deflection was too high. Furthermore, his wingman, Lt Abd el-Baki, was unable to follow his leader's very sharp turn and found himself isolated. As they left the combat zone the three undamaged Mirages downed el-Baki's isolated MiG-21. Clearly, the Egyptian pilots still had much to learn.

On 14 April Israeli Mirages claimed to have destroyed two MiG-21s, although this was later reduced to one. In fact one Egyptian MiG, flown by Ismail Imam, was damaged and returned safely. The result of the first reconnaissance of northern and southern Sinai by Egyptian Su-7s, defended by MiG-21s, ended with the Egyptians claiming one enemy jet shot down. In his recollections of the combat, Samir Aziz Mikhail stated;

Two EAF MiG-21F-13s of the élite No 26 Sqn, known as the 'Black Ravens', depart on a patrol in the early 1970s. Both aircraft are armed with R-3S missiles. Although the oldest version in service, the MiG-21F-13 was appreciated by its pilots because it was armed with a cannon, which was vital in air combat – especially as the early-generation 'Atoll' missiles so often failed (*EAF via Tom Cooper*)

Samir Aziz Mikhail, an Egyptian Christian, was one of Egypt's most experienced MiG-21 fighter pilots with two confirmed kills and one damaged to his credit. He is seen here in the cockpit of a MiG-21MF, probably around 1973 (*EAF*)

'When the GCI says they are three kilometres (two miles) behind, my knees begin to shake – the first time I am afraid. If I get shot down I will be captured. At this point I get mad and make a very steep break to the right. Then a missile explodes between me and my wingman (whose aircraft was damaged). He escapes west. I see a circle – Mirage-MiG-Mirage-MiG – but I am alone. As I've survived this long I'll try to hit one of their aircraft. I cross the circle and pick out a Mirage. He thinks I have a cannon so breaks to avoid my attack. The circle of jets fragments and everyone splits. One of the Mirages turns away. I put my gunsight on him and fire my "Atoll". A hit in the tail and a big flash! I couldn't believe it.'

One of the most unexpected outcomes came on 19 May when an Egyptian MiG-19 flown by Lt Ashir Rami shot down a Mirage. Ashir Rami was, in fact, returning from a training 'mock combat' when he came across a pair of enemy fighters near his home airfield. The Israelis promptly dropped their tanks and shot at the MiG-19 from head-on, but only two of the shells struck Ashir's left wing. The Israelis now attempted to get onto the MiG-19's tail so that they could launch their missiles. Rami had already used his missiles in training. Instead of escaping, the MiG-19 pilot engaged the two Mirages in a dogfight, and the wingman's Mirage was soon in Ashir Rami's gunsight. The Egyptian made a gentle corrective turn, increased his engine's thrust, closed to 975 ft (300 m) and fired a two-second burst which blew the Mirage apart. The Israeli leader ignited his afterburner and fled.

Two days later Mirages claimed the downing of three MiG-21s, subsequently reduced to one, although two were in fact destroyed. However, the UARAF got some revenge when a flight of No 25 Sqn MiG-21s caught the Mirages as they re-crossed the canal. Leading the Egyptians was Maj Mani, an experienced pilot who intercepted the jets on virtually a collision course. This enabled the pilots to tuck themselves beneath their enemies' tails. Mani's pair accelerated, climbed and launched two missiles at a range of 4000 ft (1300 m). One hit the jet pipe of a Mirage and the pilot ejected. He landed in the canal and was drowned.

More than three weeks of relative calm was shattered on 17 June 1969 when low-flying Israeli jets used their sonic booms to smash the windows of President Nasser's home. This supposedly resulted in Shalabi el-Hinnawy resigning as CO of the UARAF, to be replaced by Ali Mustafa Baghdadi. In reality, Hinnawy's period as commander, focussing attention on reorganisation and intensive training, had come to a close, and he was replaced by an aggressive leader whose function was to fight.

MiG-21PFS deliveries added little to the Egyptians' existing punch. Improved manoeuvrability and range helped offset the jet's continued lack of cannon, but meant that without local modifications to its armament, the MiG-21PFS remained ineffective as a dogfighter. But booster

An extremely rare photograph of an Egyptian fighter and its pilot during the War of Attrition. The aircraft is one of the first MiG-21MFs delivered in late 1969, and it displays the 'tiger stripe' camouflage applied to some Egyptian aircraft during this period. The fighter's serial number, as well as the pilot's face, have been carefully obscured, although the jet's number was probably 8472 or 8473 (*D Nicolle collection*)

This Egyptian Air Force MiG-21PFM, serial number 6154, of No 45 Sqn displays the camouflage pattern widely used in the late 1960s and early 1970s (*J W via Tom Cooper*)

Photographs of Egyptian aircraft during the War of Attrition are extremely rare. This MiG-21PFM (SPS) was probably photographed around 1969, and it displays a locally-applied camouflage scheme using car paint, as adopted by UARAF aircraft immediately after the Six Day War. Again, all identification marks have been carefully scratched out on the photograph, but enough remains of the serial number to suggest that it might be 8067. The small erased marking ahead of the serial number may have been an early version of the élite No 26 'Black Raven' Sqn insignia. The airfield is almost certainly in the Nile Delta (*D Nicolle collection*)

rockets beneath the fuselage enabled the Egyptians to develop their own ambush tactics. These involved ferrying MiG-21s by night beneath Mi-6 helicopters to rarely-used airfields and airstrips close to the Suez Canal. From here they could emerge to make sudden attacks on intruders.

Later in 1969 the UARAF took delivery of the MiG-21PFM (SPS), which did have a gun pod with a 23 mm cannon to supplement the earlier MiG-21FLs and PFs. According to Alaa Barakat, 110 MiG-21MFs also arrived in late 1969, and these were allocated to several units during 1970. These deliveries also enabled the UARAF to resolve its mixture of different MiG-21 versions. Finally, the MiG-21MF gave the Egyptians an interceptor capable of meeting Israeli Mirages on roughly equal terms.

Meanwhile, the Egyptians had developed their own strategy and tactics beyond the rudimentary skills taught by their Warsaw Pact advisers. The UARAF's role was primarily to support the EADF in countering Israeli air attacks, as well as protecting a belt of SAM sites. It also raided Israeli-occupied territory. The Egyptian command had established a primitive visual search system similar to the Royal Observer Corps in World War 2.

Largely illiterate soldiers manned outposts deep in the desert, and rolled the inductor of a field telephone if they heard an aircraft. A light

would then flicker on a vertical map at the headquarters of the SAM unit at the local air base. Another system of lights marked the progress of Egyptian aircraft on the map. But if the desert observers did not receive regular food and water, they tended to set the lights flickering randomly! When Fuad Kamal became a senior fighter controller in the Central Air Defence Operations Room late in 1969, there was a similarly old fashioned Battle of Britain-style table-top situation map, plus the vertical map which plotted the positions of friendly and hostile aircraft.

Interceptions by MiG-21s took place at high altitude, following Soviet tactics, at some distance from Egyptian SAM sites. After the SAMs were launched, the Israeli formations were usually scattered. This gave the MiGs a chance to pounce. But Egyptian MiG-21 pilots also developed low-level interception tactics based upon those employed by the Israelis.

Of particular danger to Egyptian MiG-21 pilots was the revived Israeli 'free hunting' tactic. Elite IDF/AF pilots used their Mirages' technological superiority, combined with the limitations of Egyptian radar coverage at low altitude, to prowl around Egyptian bases and catch returning MiGs. Advanced US equipment supplied to Israel made things even more difficult for the MiG-21s. More than once the Egyptians launched four or six aircraft against formations which appeared small on the radar, only to find themselves outnumbered after it was too late to avoid combat. In fact, Egyptian pilots learned that their best hope was to engage the enemy regardless, since the Israelis were extremely sensitive to losses.

Israel does not seem to have considered the possibility of a direct Soviet reaction to its humiliation of Soviet military technology and political support. Consequently, the USSR's decision to send large numbers of Soviet air defence personnel to Egypt came as a surprise. This was Operation *Kavkaz* which, agreed in principle in late 1969, resulted in over 10,000 Soviet troops arriving in Egypt during 1970. Furthermore, their weaponry included the latest SAMs and several MiG fighter units.

By March 1970 several Soviet air defence brigades had reached operational status, although the first clash between Soviet SAMs and Israeli aircraft did not happen until 30 June. Four days earlier, another combat had resulted from Israeli 'hunting' tactics near an Egyptian air base. Two MiG-21s were shot down on final approach but both pilots ejected safely. No 102 Air Brigade also lost a MiG-21 in combat over the Gulf of Suez, although Tamim Fahmi Abd Allah's account differed from that published by the Israelis. He reported;

'We ran to the jeep, drove to the aircraft and scrambled. My wingman and I tuned to the operations channel and they directed us to intercept the enemy in an effort to support the other Inshas fighters. I saw a Mirage all by himself heading back east. I tried to dive to catch him. At about one mile away he turned hard into me, but I didn't have a gun so I manoeuvred with him. He was turning hard and I did a high-speed yo-yo to keep with him. We did this about three times, then he reversed and dived. I went below him to get a missile tone. I heard the buzz of the "Atoll" and I thought it was good. The missile went out, exploded near him and I saw smoke.'

Mirages then appeared at an altitude of 13,000 ft (4000 m) on Egyptian radars. As they flew along the canal, they came close to the base of the élite No 26 'Black Ravens' Sqn, so the Egyptians sent up an interception flight of their most experienced pilots. They scrambled without drop-tanks, as

Fuad Kamal commanded the most experienced Egyptian MiG-21 pilots who had been selected for a new 'big squadron' formed at Cairo West during the final days of the Six Day War. Fuad remained in command for two months, then became the UARAF's Chief Fighter Inspector. He is now one of Egypt's leading portrait painters (*Fuad Kama*)

these reduced speed, and consequently Egyptian ground controllers needed to vector them into an attack position very precisely. The sortie went according to plan and the four climbing MiG-21F-13s caught the Israelis as they turned away from the SAM batteries. The rear Mirage pair was shot down almost simultaneously. But this success was overshadowed by the loss of the wingman from the second Egyptian pair, who had to eject when he ran out of fuel.

This was probably the combat when Ahmad Nur el-Din made his third victory claim by shooting down a Mirage over Lake Manzalah. After it was over, he told his friends that he felt 'strangely bad' because the Mirage pilot seemed very inexperienced and made many mistakes.

On the night of 19-20 July 1969, Israeli commandos destroyed a radar position on Green Island to punch a breach in Egyptian radar coverage. Israeli fighters swarmed through in a sustained series of raids against anti-aircraft defences. The UARAF struck back immediately, and the 20th saw the largest air battle since the Six Day War. When it was over, IDF/AF pilots claimed five Egyptian aircraft downed and admitted the loss of two Mirages, one to a MiG-21. In turn, the Egyptians admitted two losses but claimed two Mirages in air combat. In fact Israeli aircraft shot down at least one (and possibly two) of their own Mirages during a combat with Kadri el-Hamid and his wingman in a dense dust haze over Hurghada.

On 9 September another Israeli commando raid destroyed small Egyptian outposts along 40 miles (60 km) of coast south of Suez on Egypt's side of the Red Sea. The Egyptians had to respond, and on 11 September 102 of their aircraft launched a major raid. The planners hoped Israeli air defences would be blinded by the destruction of several radars. This did not work out in practice, and the ground-attack aircraft met stiff resistance. As a result, Egyptian MiG-21 interceptors had to be thrown in to defend the MiG-17s and Su-7s.

The most significant aerial battle took place over Fayid between four Egyptian MiG-21s and eight Israeli Mirages. Maj Fawzi Salama's flight attacked despite being outnumbered. Salama first engaged the enemy leader and, as a member of the Egyptian Air Force aerobatic team, soon used his proven abilities as a pilot to gain the advantage, shooting down the Israeli as he tried to break away. Fawzi Salama's victim was ace Giora Rom. The Israelis also lost another élite pilot named Weintraub who was downed by Samir Aziz Mikhail flying a No 104 Air Brigade MiG-21FL.

On the 11th the UARAF reportedly lost five MiG-21s, plus three other aircraft. But the day ended on a brighter note when young Lt Ghema found himself 'in the right place at the right time' as the result of a navigational error while ferrying a MiG-21. He was making his final approach

A MiG-21F-13 of the élite No 26 'Black Ravens' Sqn. The unit was based at Sayah el-Sharif in 1969, although this photograph was probably taken the following year, since the aircraft displays the EAF's new national markings (*Russian Military Archives*)

Egyptian MiG-21 pilot Ahmad Nur el-Din was confirmed as having shot down three enemy aircraft and one probable, but most of these victories are disputed by the Israelis. Nur el-Din was killed when he had to eject over Egypt's mountainous Eastern Desert at very low altitude on 2 July 1969, having run his fighter out of fuel (*EAF*)

when ground control told him to go round again. After flying a full circuit at low level, Ghema suddenly found himself behind a Mirage which was lining up on the tail of another MiG as it came in to land. The Israeli was slightly below him, so Ghema risked throttling his engine back to minimum and closing to within 3000 ft (1000 m) of the Mirage's tail. The Israeli pilot was preoccupied with his intended victim, and Israeli radar could not warn him since both aircraft were beneath its coverage. Ghema fired two missiles which struck their target. Capt Jacob Roum ejected and was taken prisoner, suffering multiple injuries.

The Israelis continued their attacks while UARAF raids also increased. The air war was involving increased use of electronic counter measures (ECM). On the night of 7-8 November the Egyptian Navy launched a daring coastal bombardment of Israeli targets in north-western Sinai. It was a resounding success. The attack also drew in MiG-21 nightfighters, one of which was flown by Samir Aziz Mikhail, who recalled;

'I saw flares and I was told by the fighter controller that there were four aircraft making air-to-sea attacks – I didn't know we had ships there. So I caught one aircraft on the radar, but at this moment I heard a noise on the radio. They were jamming my radio frequency with the controller very loudly. And then the flares stopped. The aircraft on my radar dived and I lost the contact in the clutter.'

On 27 November a major air battle erupted 25 miles (40 km) inside Sinai. Apparently, the MiGs were incorrectly vectored and found themselves in front of the Israeli fighters. Furthermore, Egyptian ground control was so effectively jammed by Israeli ECM that pilots could not be warned. However, on 9 December Egypt took its revenge when Ahmed Atef became the UARAF's first Phantom II 'killer', having already been in combat with Israeli Mirages earlier in the day. Two Mirages were spotted by one of the EADF's new Russian P-15 low-altitude radars.

For once the Egyptians had a technological advantage, the Israeli pilots having switched off their airborne radars so as to remain electronically invisible. The pair of MiG-21s popped up on a head-on collision course and opened fire with 23 mm guns. The surprised Israelis made a climbing combat turn and lost sight of the MiGs which, beneath them now, launched their missiles. Both Mirages were shot down.

That evening a section of MiG-21s, flown by Sami Marei, Mohamed Ismail Oweis, Ahmed Atef and Moneir Hamdi, was sent to the area between the Gabal Ataka and Sukhna to stop enemy fighters supporting a reconnaissance aircraft which had been intercepted by other MiGs. A large scale dogfight ensued as Atef and Moneir closed with Israeli Phantom IIs at low altitude. The pilot of leading F-4 ignited his afterburner and dived to the left. His wingman appeared to have suffered damage, however, and fell behind the main group, trailing smoke. It proved quite easy for the Egyptian to deliver the final blow. Atef closed in and went lower so the heat from the ground would not affect his missiles. The first 'Atoll' exploded under the Phantom II's tail pipe and the second inside it, forcing the crew to eject. Ahmed Atef's score was increased to four victories, most of which were denied by Israeli sources.

Such Egyptian successes were rare and, according to the records of the Soviet advisory mission, the UARAF lost 72 combat aircraft between July 1969 and the end of the year. Of these, 29 had been due to accidents and other non-combat losses, leaving 53 MiGs, Sukhois and Ilyushins shot down by anti-aircraft fire, SAMs or Israeli fighters. Soviet sources stated that the Israelis had lost just under half that number in 1968-69.

On 8 February 1970 Israeli Phantom IIs attacked Egyptians airfields and, because of the highly sophisticated ECM and other equipment that they now carried, suffered little loss. There was, however, a major clash over the Delta resulting in the downing of one F-4E and perhaps two MiG-21s. The next day the Israelis admitted the loss of a Mirage to a MiG-21. The Egyptians claimed two Mirage IIs, one to Lt Urfan, with the pilot (Avinoam Keldes) being captured, and another to Lt Ismail.

On 26 February four MiG-21s took off from the road-strip at Quwaysina, Maj Sami Marei leading 1Lt Mohamed Oweis, Ahmed Atef and Ibrahim Hamad. Their target was four Mirages flying west of Ismailiya, but they also encountered eight Phantom IIs. The MiG-21s broke formation to stop the approaching F-4s, with Marei taking on two, although he was soon surrounded. Mohamed Oweis suggested his commander should eject, but Marei refused, having always told his men that the aircraft was part of the pilot. Shortly afterwards he was killed.

Other combats were recorded over the following days, with the Israelis claiming a further nine MiGs. These claims were inflated, but there was no doubt that the UARAF was suffering serious losses. So it was a great relief when a substantial force of Soviet air force MiG-21MFs arrived in Egypt. They took over Beni Sueif air base, and with it the defence of Egypt south of Cairo, which enabled the Egyptians to send several units north.

On 8 April a massive Israeli air-raid hit a school in the eastern Delta region, killing 46 children. This, and the fact that Israeli aircraft almost clashed with Soviet-flown MiG-21s, resulted in Israeli deep penetration raids being called off. The war's focus moved back to the Suez Canal. Egyptian interceptor squadrons could now support an increase in UARAF offensive raids.

During the final days of May 1970, the IDF/AF launched a major air assault against Port Said, apparently under the impression that the Egyptians were assembling an amphibious landing force there. On the 16th an Israeli jet was certainly shot down in air combat – probably by a MiG-21 – bringing admitted Israeli losses on the Egyptian front to

UARAF MiG-21 pilot Lt Ismail tells a press conference on 11 February 1970 how he shot down an Israeli Mirage two days earlier. Egypt claimed two victories on the 9th, although the Israelis admitted only one loss (*EAF*)

This MiG-21MF, flown by the Soviet 135th Air Regiment in Egypt in 1970-71, displays the camouflage scheme applied at the Gorky factory in Russia. These aircraft received Egyptian national markings and serial numbers, 8692 in this case (*Russian military Archives*)

A pair of Soviet-flown MiG-21MFs of the 135th Air Regiment boast full Egyptian UARAF markings and the serial numbers 7303 and 7304 at Beni Sueif in 1970 (*authors' collections*)

36 aircraft and one helicopter. On 8 June Egypt announced that two MiG-21 pilots, Fikri el-Ashmawy and Rauf el-Din, had each downed an F-4E, probably referring to a major attack the previous day. According to Israeli sources, a single A-4 Skyhawk was also lost in air combat in June 1970, falling east of the Canal on the 20th after being attacked by a pair of MiG-21MFs, which were then shot down by Mirages.

When Soviet aircraft failed to challenge Israeli raids near the Canal, the IDF/AF decided to test their willingness to fight. Several jets ventured beyond the Canal zone, and each time Soviet fighters were launched the Israelis withdrew. On 23 June Israeli commandos attacked an outpost close to the Soviet base at Beni Sueif. Although they aircraft did not intervene, they did push their MiG-21 patrols closer to the Canal. At the same time Egyptian and Soviet air defence personnel pushed forward several SAM and anti-aircraft batteries. Two F-4Es were promptly shot down.

Meanwhile, the UARAF launched air raids across the Canal, usually by Su-7s protected by MiG-21s. On 27 June eight aircraft struck Israeli rear areas in Sinai. The IDF/AF claimed to have downed two MiG-17s, but admitted the loss of a Mirage in air combat. Its pilot was captured, but died ten days later in an Egyptian military hospital. On 30 June there was a further clash between MiG-21s and Phantom IIs, and Capt Naseem Faid was wounded when a cannon shell shattered his helmet. Meanwhile, F-4s and A-4s were now falling at a steady rate, mostly to SAMs or flak.

On 23 July 1970 Nasser announced his acceptance of an American-sponsored cease-fire proposal, followed just over a week later by the Israeli government. The cease-fire came into effect on 8 August.

During 17 months of combat in 1969-70 there had been 50 battles over the canal, during which, according to Soviet sources, some 60 Egyptian and 30 Israeli aircraft had been downed – at least nine of the latter by fighters. The Israelis admitted losing 30 aircraft during the entire period between the Six Day War and the 1970 cease-fire – only four were supposedly air combat losses. More significantly, perhaps, losses were running at roughly an equal rate during the final phase of the War of Attrition.

President Nasser died of a heart attack on 28 September 1970. Vice President Anwar Sadat took over, but took time to consolidate his authority. Furthermore, the Soviets refused to supply Egypt with modern military equipment. By 1972 there was a widespread feeling in the air force that the quality of Soviet advisers had declined. In June Sadat decided that it was time for them to go. The result was their hasty and undignified departure in a fleet of An-12, An-22, Il-18 and Il-62 transports, as well as ships. About 100 technical and electronics advisers remained, however.

For a while the Soviet departure was believed to have weakened Egyptian military potential, particularly in the air. In reality, morale steadily improved and the air force quietly filled the gaps left by the disappearance

Soviet Air Force Maj Valerie Yel'chaninov is seen in an Egyptian Air Force dual-control MiG-21UM, probably in early 1970 (*authors' collections*)

Air Marshal Shafik, Egyptian Air Force CO, pictured in 1997. As a young MiG-21 pilot, he became an expert in the low-level 'sniper' interception tactics developed by the Egyptians towards the end of the War of Attrition, and was confirmed as having shot down at least one Skyhawk. He subsequently commanded a MiG-21 squadron during the October 1973 War (*EAF*)

A pair of Soviet 135th Air Regiment MiG-21MFs in Egyptian UARAF markings fly over Egypt in 1970 (*authors collections*)

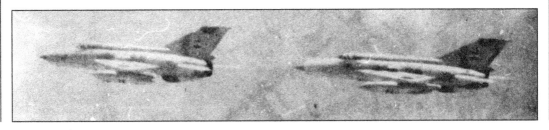

Egyptian MiG-21 pilot Naseem Faid fought in the War of Attrition and was wounded on 30 June 1970 when a cannon shell fired by an Israeli Phantom II shattered his helmet (*EAF*)

Although presented as a 'combat photograph', this remarkable picture of an Egyptian MiG-21MF pursuing a Mirage over the desert was probably taken during training in the early 1970s, possibly against a Libyan or Pakistani-flown Libyan aircraft (*Russian Military Archive*)

of their Soviet friends. By October 1973, some 390 Egyptian pilots were qualified to fly the MiG-21 or Su-7. Anticipated losses of one per 100 sorties in 1970 were down to one per 500 by the end of 1972, largely due to improved ECM and more experience in handling new equipment.

Several pilots were also sent to train in Pakistan and Libya, where they gained Mirage experience. A few Pakistani instructors originally seconded to Libya also came to Egypt, where they taught air combat instructors ultra-slow and extremely tight-turning manoeuvres developed by their air force. According to Nabil Shoukry, the Pakistanis then asked the Egyptians not to demonstrate these manoeuvres to the Soviet advisers, because they feared the information would be passed onto the Indians.

Hosni Mubarak took over from Ali Mustafa Baghdadi as air force CO in April 1972. By then the force was again designated the Egyptian Air Force (EAF), the redundant UARAF title having been dropped. New national markings were also applied to the aircraft.

The situation along the cease-fire lines between Israeli and Egyptian forces would remain generally quiet after the departure of Soviet forces, but on 13 June 1972 two Phantom IIs penetrated Egyptian airspace south of Port Said and were pursued by a pair of MiG-21s from Mansourah. Within minutes the MiGs had been ambushed by eight Israeli aircraft over the Mediterranean and both were shot down.

SYRIA AND IRAQ

The Six Day War was a shattering experience for all Arab air forces. It was clear that the pilots' valour was wasted because of inadequate organisation and equipment. Unlike the Egyptians, however, Syrian and Iraqi leadership failed to face reality. Consequently, poor conduct of operations and a lack of sufficient planning and coordination, combined with poor intelligence estimates, remained characteristic of missions undertaken by Syrian and Iraqi MiG-19 and MiG-21 units after the 1967 war.

Several years passed before the Syrians accepted that only a highly professional and perfectly prepared force was capable of standing its ground in future confrontations. It was also clear that training had to be

An Egyptian MiG-21 in newly-painted EAF national markings in 1971-72. The aircraft (serial number 8038) still has the simple 'sand and spinach' camouflage added after the Six Day War. Note that it also has a new, and as yet unpainted, cockpit canopy frame
(*Russian Military Archives*)

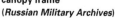

intensified and improved to enable Syrian pilots to face the Israelis. In Iraq too, many senior officers simply refused to admit what had happened to Arab air forces. On the contrary, the IrAF higher echelons continued to engage in domestic political rivalries, resulting in much damage. And despite being essential to the success of the Ba'athist coup in 1968, the IrAF was again purged in 1971. Consequently, it could not participate in the prolonged clashes with Israel which became known as the War of Attrition.

Although the Syrians did not overhaul their air force to the same extent as the Egyptians, they did occasionally engage Israeli aircraft. By late 1968, SyAAF Six Day War losses had been replaced and the force was now larger. No new MiG-19s were purchased, but instead over 60 MiG-21s were organised in five operational units, while the total number of units operating this type would increase as additional squadrons were re-equipped. The 8th, 10th and 11th Sqns were still flying MiG-21F-13s which remained the most numerous variant in Syrian service. The 67th and 68th Sqns eventually replaced their MiG-17s with MiG-21F-13s, while the 5th and 9th were re-equipped with MiG-21PFs. Finally, the 77th replaced its MiG-19s with MiG-21PFs. By 1968 all remaining Syrian and Iraqi MiG-19s had been sent to Egypt.

During the War of Attrition, most engagements between Israeli and Syrian aircraft resulted from staged and well-planned operations in which each side tried to exploit the advantages of its aircraft and, in the case of the Israelis, the experience of its best pilots. All were fast and furious, with both sides, especially the less experienced Syrians, suffering considerable losses. However, the Syrians were always capable of hitting back, despite their aircraft being badly outgunned, often lacking functional weapons and possessing only modest range and payload capacity compared to Israel's Mirages and Phantom IIs. It was, for example, Syrian MiG-21 pilot Capt Bassam Hamshu who was the first Arab to down an Israeli F-4E on 2 April 1970. Considering the total number of engagements against Israeli fighters, Syrian pilots often shot down more aircraft than the Egyptians.

Despite the cease-fire between Egypt and Israel becoming effective in August 1970, the situation over the Golan Heights never quietened. Although the Israeli political leadership was confident that there would be no Arab counter-attack before 1974, the IDF/AF constantly monitored Syrian positions with its RF-4E Phantom II reconnaissance aircraft. The biggest problem for the Israelis was that the Syrians were adept at covering their positions with camouflage. But, under pressure from Soviet advisers, they seldom activated electronic emissions.

In most cases, the Phantom IIs were fast enough to leave enemy territory zones before Syrian interceptors could arrive. However, at around 1400 hrs on 13 September 1973, two RF-4Es and two F-4Es approaching the Syrian coast between Latakia and Tartus almost fell into a trap. The Syrians had suddenly deployed several P-12 radars

Syrian Air Force Capt Bassam Hamshu was the first Arab fighter pilot to shoot down an Israeli F-4 Phantom II, the jet crashing into the foothills of Mount Hermon on 2 April 1970. The 5th Sqn's Hamshu was flying a MiG-21, and he eventually became the highest scoring Arab fighter ace with seven confirmed aerial and one strafing victories. He was shot down and killed by Israeli F-15As on 6 June 1982 (*SyAAF*)

The wreckage of the Israeli F-4E Phantom II shot down by pilot Capt Bassam Hamshu on 2 April 1970 (*SyAAF*)

in this area, and the Israeli formation was detected early. Four 54th Sqn MiG-21PFs, forward-deployed at Abu al-Dahur airfield, were immediately scrambled and vectored to intercept. The two RF-4Es, escorted from a distance by four Mirage IIICs, seem to have planned to cross the coast north of Tartus and then turn south to evade Syrian defences. But over the coast they were bounced by the MiGs led by Capt Adeeb el-Gar. The Israelis promptly aborted the mission, the Phantom IIs turning west, engaging afterburners and flying very low with the MiGs in pursuit.

Flying at the head of his formation, el-Gar was the first in position to fire two missiles. At least one exploded close enough to the target to make it crash into the sea. At that moment, the escorting Mirage IIICs and Neshers appeared above and pounced on Syrian formation. The highly-experienced Israeli pilots had no difficulty in gaining the upper hand in a brief dogfight, two MiGs being shot down – neither pilot ejected.

Meanwhile, another four MiG-21s, led by Capt Magar, were approaching the area. Shortly after crossing the coast near Tartus, they reported visual contact with the combat, but then the formation was itself jumped by four Mirages. Two MiGs, including that flown by the CO, were shot down within seconds. The remaining two Syrians engaged the Israelis and fired several R-13M missiles before another MiG was shot down. The fourth Syrian pilot, Capt al-Halabi, destroyed the Mirage flown by Yossi Shimchoni, who ejected and came down in the sea near the Lebanese coast not far from one of the three downed Syrian pilots.

Almost an hour later, the IDF/AF despatched a CH-53D helicopter, escorted by sections of Phantom IIs and Mirages, to rescue the downed pilot. But two further sections of MiG-21FLs appeared, one being led by Capt el-Gar on his second mission of the day. One section tried to intercept the CH-53D while el-Gar and his wingmen closed undetected beneath several Phantom IIs and hit one with a missile. During this combat, Israeli Mirages and Neshers claimed three MiGs, with a fourth damaged. In total, the Israelis claimed 12 kills and one probable for one loss that day. Damascus admitted five losses, but claimed eight Israeli aircraft, including two F-4Es downed by Capt el-Gar, who was subsequently promoted. After the October War he was awarded the Hero of the Republic Medal for 'destroying two Phantom IIs in air combat over Beirut'.

Between 1968 and 1972 Arab MiG-21 pilots had to re-learn the art of air combat – how to turn their aircraft despite heavy stick forces using flaps, and discover the best attack and defence manoeuvres. This could not be done overnight. Nor was it to be found in their manuals, since the Soviets were not teaching such skills. In fact, Arab pilots re-wrote the manuals for the MiG-21, learning lessons for which they paid in blood.

While Arab pilots went through this learning process without effective outside help, they simultaneously tried to hit back against Israel to bolster the morale which had been shattered by the Six Day War. Pilots had to learn to fly and fight at low levels and low speeds, and to use their weapons properly while still employing basically the same equipment as was available in 1967. Despite such problems, Arab pilots flew and fought regardless of cost. They even protested whenever high commands ordered them to refrain from combat. It cannot be denied that Arab MiG-21 pilots – Egyptians, Syrians, Iraqis, Algerians and Jordanians among them – had an amazing amount of what in pilot-jargon is known simply as 'guts'.

SURPRISING EVEN THEMSELVES

Egypt was now divided into six air defence zones, each with its own control centre and attached radar battalions. A seventh, designated Zone 1, was the occupied Sinai peninsula, and existed only as a nameplate, Zone 2 covered the north-east from Port Said along the Suez Canal and Gulf of Suez as far south as Ras Zafaranah, with its HQ at Abu Suweir. Zone 3, or the Central Sector, had its HQ in Cairo, Zone 4, with its HQ at Alexandria, covered the western fringes of the Nile Delta and the Western Desert, Zone 5 had its HQ at Aswan, and covered southern Egypt as well as vast areas of desert to the east and west, Zone 6 covered the central Nile Delta from its HQ at Mansourah, and Zone 7 covered a desert area south-east of Egypt from the Gulf of Suez along the Red Sea coast as far as the Sudanese frontier, with its HQ at Hurghada. A planned Zone 8 would have encompassed a huge swathe of the Sahara desert as far as the Libyan and Sudanese frontiers from an HQ at Beni Sueif.

Before the 1973 October War, the EAF was still organised in Soviet-style air brigades, with three operational MiG-21 brigades having their headquarters at Mansourah, Inshas and Luxor, and a fourth MiG-21 operational training brigade being based at Gabal el-Basur. Between six and nine interceptor squadrons, equipped with various versions of MiG-21, were integrated with the EADF Command, while others were primarily intended to protect the ground-attack squadrons. There was also a tactical reconnaissance flight equipped with MiG-21RFs.

Available sources differ considerably in their estimates of the number of MiG-21s actually available to the EAF at the start of the October 1973 war, and range from 150 to 260 aircraft, including unserviceable machines. Each unit was supposed to have 12 MiG-21s, not counting reserve aircraft or those in store. Some sources maintain that no MiG-19s remained in active service, while others claim the EAF still had up to 120, with 60 actually in service. Inshas was the main centre for MiG-21 repair, although there were limited maintenance facilities at other bases. One helicopter squadron was allocated to search and rescue duties.

The large number of reserve landing grounds and road-strips also offered reassurance, given the MiG-21's tendency to run out of fuel after air combat. The old air base at Fayid, on the western shore of the great Bitter Lake, may have also been available in an emergency.

This frame from a roll of 16 mm news film shows an Egyptian MiG-21MF in full afterburner in 1971. The aircraft displays an early version of the three-colour 'Nile' camouflage developed in Egypt (*D Nicolle collection*)

For Egyptian pilots, the 1973
October War opened with hundreds
of attack-sorties against targets on
the Sinai peninsula. This EAF
MiG-21MF can be seen shortly after
take-off, armed with four Egyptian-
designed and manufactured
runway-piercing 'dibber' bombs
(*Tom Cooper collection*)

In the months and weeks leading up to the October war, allied air units arrived from a variety of countries. Iraqi Hunters were based at Mansourah, Pakistani instructors at Inshas reportedly flew combat missions in Egyptian MiG-21s, and others are said to have flown Libyan Mirages at Mansourah. The Algerian (QJA) contingent in Egypt included two squadrons of MIG-21F-13s and PFs, all units being under the command of Mohamed Tahar Bouzroub. A QJA forward headquarters had, in fact, been established in Egypt as early as 1970, although Algerian MiG-21s remained in Libya until early October 1973. With its chronic shortage of MiG-21 pilots, the EAF was also happy to accept a small North Korean contingent of experienced men, many with over 2000 flying hours. The group reached Egypt in June, and included 20 pilots, eight controllers, five interpreters, three administrators a doctor and a cook.

Before the October war, all main Israeli targets are said to have been re-created in the Libyan desert so that EAF pilots could practice ground-attack sorties against them. In its ground-attack mode, the MiG-21 carried two 500- or four 250-kg bombs or four rocket pods. During the 1973 conflict, No 102 Fighter Air Wing participated in the first strike, and then defended the Delta air bases in cooperation with No 104 Air Wing, which escorted EAF fighter-bombers during the first strike.

Egyptian aircraft planned to return from attack missions around the northern and southern flanks of the dense belt of SAMs and anti-aircraft artillery which protected the western bank of the Suez Canal. Following the Egyptian air offensive, most MiG-21s were held back in the knowledge that the IDF/AF would attempt to knock out the EAF's bases. At the start of the October war, Egypt had over 400 early warning, target acquisition and fire control radars, but still used observers for visual detection of low-level penetrations.

EAF interception techniques along the canal front involved sending mis-sile-armed MiG-21MFs against high altitude intruders or those at extreme range. SAMs were for medium altitude defence, backed up if necessary by MiG-21MFs. The risk of friendly fire incidents was considered acceptable. Low-level intruders would be engaged by anti-aircraft guns, although MiGs were often sent against them too. In defence of their own bases, MiG-21s rarely flew standing patrols because they were vulnerable to Israeli ambush tactics. Instead, pilots stood on high alert and could achieve very short scramble times. In addition to the old-fashioned observer corps, the EAF used a similarly archaic, but effective, system of barrage balloons which ringed some bases at a height of 1600 ft (500 m).

The EAF employed interception tactics, but at middle or lower altitude pilots would usually attack from below and split enemy formations, because only one Israeli aircraft would typically carry ECM equipment for the group. Once divided, the enemy formation became vulnerable to attack by SAMs or radar-guided anti-aircraft artillery.

For Egypt, Zero Hour was set at 1400 hrs on 6 October 1973. EAF pilots were informed at 1230 hrs. Engines were started while aircraft were still inside their hardened hangers, and the plan was to get 220 jets over their targets virtually simultaneously. This initial assault lasted approximately 15 minutes, and the first wave met no aerial opposition. There was no radar or communications jamming by the enemy either. In fact, the Egyptians achieved complete surprise. MiG-21s provided fighter cover for Su-7s and

One of the first targets attacked by the EAF on 6 October 1973 was Bir Gifgafah air base, known to the Israelis as Refidim. These Egyptian MiG-21 gun-camera photographs show the main runway under attack. Two black circles drawn on the shot below show craters in the runway caused by Egyptian 'dibber' bombs. Several Israeli aircraft were also reportedly destroyed on the ground by cannon fire (*EAF*)

MiG-17 fighter-bombers, although some were also used in the ground-attack role. The last attacking aircraft crossed the Suez Canal at 1420 hrs. Only one aircraft and four helicopters had been lost. A planned second strike was cancelled because the first had been so successful. The EAF also claimed that the air bases hit in Sinai remained inoperative for 48 hours.

It was a day of triumph and even revenge for the participants, whether or not they actually flew combat missions. One pilot who attacked southern Sinai was Dia el-Hefnawy of the No 25 Sqn detachment sent to Hurghada ten days before the war began. The other half remained at Inshas with No 26 Sqn, while No 27 was at Abu Hammad. Dia's first duty was to protect MiG-17s attacking Ras Nasrani air base, but the MiG-21s did not themselves take part in the ground attack. Nor did they meet any aerial opposition.

Moustafa Hafiz was CO of a MiG-21MF unit based at Inshas. He said;

'I led my squadron in the initial attack on Bir Thamadah (Milayz) airfield. Our MiG-21MFs used anti-runway bombs, and we flew a low-level attack. However, on the way in I had to increase altitude at least twice as we flew towards Bir Thamadah because the MiG-17s were attacking the Hawk sites – I had to climb up to 150-200 m (500-650 ft) so as not to obstruct their attacks. With a "dibber" bomb you don't have to aim – you just fly along the runway and let them go.'

The last EAF sortie of the day flown was by a pair of MiG-21RFs.

This MiG-21MF, believed to be Egyptian, is captured on film rolling over an Israeli position at very low level against a background of explosions from bombs dropped by other MiGs. Egyptian and Syrian pilots became highly proficient at low-level flying in the MiG-21 (*Tom Cooper collection*)

This IDF/AF F-4E was caught by the gun-camera of an Egyptian MiG-21 during one of the large-scale aerial battles fought out over the Nile Delta during the October 1973 War. The MiG-21 proved to be far more agile than the Phantom II in low-level dogfights, although its armament was far weaker (*EAF*)

This remarkable photograph was taken from an Egyptian MiG-21 gun-camera film. It shows an Israeli Mirage pursuing another Egyptian MiG-21, the former reportedly being shot down moments after this photograph was taken (*EAF*)

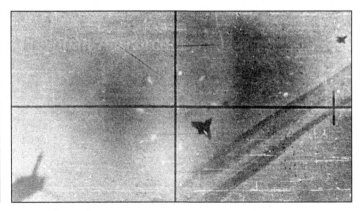

which flew down the eastern side of the canal to obtain full photographic coverage of the battle zone. By the end of day one the Egyptians admitted the loss of ten aircraft, plus some helicopters, while their air defences claimed to have destroyed 27 Israeli machines. This total was inflated, but the IDF/AF did suffer significant losses.

DAY TWO ONWARDS

The following day the Israelis attempted to stop the Egyptians extending their bridgeheads by attacking several EAF bases. This, and subsequent efforts, met with total failure. Seven waves of 40 or so aircraft swept in from the Mediterranean at low altitude, but Egyptian radar and coastal observers warned the EAF in time to allow about 60 MiG-21s to be scrambled. Few Israelis reached their targets, and a 'massive air battle' began near the Delta coast, then rolled inland, mostly at or below 20,000 ft (6150 m). The combat was rarely supersonic after the first few seconds, and was sometimes down to stalling speed. Many dogfights were also at extremely low altitude, as the Israelis tried to creep below Egyptian radar.

The assaults on the third and fourth days were also substantial, but were then called off. Kadri el-Hamid recalled the ferocity of the air fighting;

'I engaged in an air combat on 7 October during the first big air raid against us. My wingman shot down an F-4 which was right behind me with his cannon. The crew went to Mansourah hospital because they were hurt in the ejection. I also claimed a Phantom II destroyed.'

Elsewhere, Egyptian aircraft continued to launch ground-attack sorties in support of the expanding bridgehead, and MiG-21s attacked the Bar Lev fortress of 'Budapest', near Baluza. By midnight Egyptian claims had risen to 30 Israeli aircraft destroyed for the loss of six, none of which fell in air combat on the second day. Algerian aircraft were also in action, including QJA MiG-21s.

On Day Three (8 October) the Israelis attacked Mansourah and Abu Hammad (Qattamiyah) in the afternoon, but without success. Dia el-Hefnawy's half squadron returned to Inshas and 100 newly trained pilots returned from the USSR. After failing against the north-east Delta air bases, the IDF/AF tried to destroy Egyptian air defences at the northern end of the battle zone. This resulted in a major battle over Port Said. Here, the air fighting lasted five days, and was accompanied by heavy Israeli bombing. By the time the IDF/AF abandoned this effort the Egyptians had claimed 28 enemy aircraft destroyed. The EAF even reported the Israelis were shooting at their own jets in the general confusion.

Samir Aziz Mikhail was one of the MiG-21 pilots involved;

'There was a scramble and I took off and headed towards Port Said to fight with eight Mirages. We had a finger four of MiG-21MFs. Before I engaged, I told my pilots to drop their fuel tanks, but mine hung up because of an electrical failure. We started to manoeuvre, and my No 2 was dead about 30 seconds after that. My No 3 started manoeuvring with them, and I was alone with all my fuel tanks like a sitting duck. So I made a very hard turn to the right and one came in front of me. I tried the gun but it didn't work. I thought to myself, "Something is very wrong with this aircraft. The tanks won't separate, the gun doesn't work and the missiles don't fire". I knew they would kill me for sure. Everywhere I looked I saw a Mirage. So I decide to crash into one of them.'

Aziz tried this several times but failed and so somehow survived. Cairo claimed 24 enemy aircraft destroyed, plus some helicopters, at the end of Day Three, with several aircrew taken prisoner.

Egyptian soldiers proudly display part of the wing of an Israeli No 109 Sqn A-4E Skyhawk, shot down by gunfire from an EAF MiG-21MF on 7 October 1973. It fell near Shallufa, on the western side of the Suez Canal (*Egyptian MoD, via Tom Cooper*)

Early in the morning of 9 October EAF airfields at Mansourah and Abu Hammad (Qattamiyah) were attacked again. But no Egyptian aircraft were hit on the ground, and the Israelis reportedly lost 16 aircraft, with four aircrew captured. Skyhawk losses had been so high that the aircraft were taken off deep penetration raids. That day's assault would be the last against the main Egyptian air bases for a while.

On Day Five, Egyptian MiG-21s were largely held back to defend the Delta. The only Israeli attacks were against a radar site on the Mediterranean coast and the smaller airfields or road-strips at Abu Hammad and Quwaysina. Even these failed, as aircraft jettisoned their bombs and retreated before reaching their targets. Four were claimed shot down near the airfields, with two more reportedly falling near the coast. Another Israeli attack in the northern Delta in the early afternoon was intercepted. Four Phantom IIs and a Mirage were claimed for no admitted losses.

Day Six saw two EAF MiG-21PFMs from No 41 Sqn at Tanta and two MiG-21MFs of No 45 Sqn at Mansourah intercept four Israeli Skyhawks

The battered remains of a wing from an Israeli No 101 Sqn Mirage IIIC, shot down by a MiG-21 of the EAF's No 45 Sqn on 11 October 1973. The balding European in sun-glasses and a short-sleeved white shirt, centre background, is East German intelligence officer Col Otto Abel. The former MiG-17, -19 and -21 fighter pilot, and holder of an advanced engineering degree, was sent to Egypt in 1968 to study captured and recovered Western weapons systems. He also flew at least ten combat air patrols in Egyptian MiG-21MFs during the last week of the October 1973 War (*Tom Cooper collection*)

attacking an Egyptian Army supply convoy heading for the canal front. The A-4s were escorted by Mirages, which turned to confront the MiGs. One MiG-21PFM was shot down within seconds by an air-to-air missile, and shortly afterwards a MiG-21MF fell to cannon fire. The Israeli fighters attempted to disengage, but a Skyhawk had been damaged by SA-7 shoulder-launched SAMs and the surviving MiG-21s would not go away. In the resulting dogfight the MiG-21MFs downed a Mirage with gunfire, although the Israelis inevitably claimed that it had been lost to flak.

But the Arabs' strategic situation was deteriorating, and the USSR even considered sending a unit of MiG-25RBs to Egypt to attack Tel Aviv – a mission far beyond Egypt's capabilities. The aircraft were eventually sent, but no attack took place.

On Day Seven (12 October) Israeli aircraft continued their attacks around Port Said. The following day the EAF was again attacking Israeli targets in Sinai, but there was no mention of Israeli attacks on Egyptian airfields. The 13th also saw the start of a substantial Soviet airlift of military equipment to Egypt. All flights were undertaken at night and in complete radio silence. Most Soviet advisers had been ordered to leave Egypt in 1972, but now a handful of Soviet pilots returned. So too did a Soviet advisory mission to help at air regimental headquarters and operational training centres, plus a unit of four MiG-25RBs. They formed the 154th OAO (Separate Air Group) of the 47th ORAP (Independent Reconnaissance Air Regiment), whose main task was war zone reconnaissance.

Despite Egypt's deteriorating military situation, 14 October is regarded as the day of the EAF's greatest aerial victories, and was subsequently celebrated as Egyptian Air Force Day. It opened with an Israeli attack on the Port Said area at around 0100 hrs. Later, the IDF/AF launched a massive assault on EAF bases at Salihiyah, Mansourah and Tanta to destroy No 104 Air Brigade. At 1500 hrs, the brigade's alert aircraft were ready with pilots in their cockpits. Fifteen minutes later observation posts reported 20 Phantom IIs approaching from the sea near Port Said, bound for the Delta. EAF CO Hosni Mubarak ordered No 104 Air Brigade CO Gen Ahmed Abdul Rahman Nasr to scramble 16 MiG-21s to form a defensive umbrella, but not to go looking for the enemy.

Normally, the Israelis attacked in three stages, starting with a wave of fighters to draw Egyptian interceptors away from the target, followed by a suppression wave, with an escort designed to crush the Egyptian air defence. The third, or main attacking, force then headed straight for the target. In fact, the first F-4s flew in circles, then retreated across the coast.

MiG-21MF serial number 8691, pictured here in 1974, was a survivor from the October 1973 War. It still displays the original camouflage pattern applied in the Soviet Union before delivery to Egypt in the early 1970s (*Denis Hughes/AW&ST via Tom Cooper*)

At around 1530 hrs Egyptian radar detected about 60 F-4Es approaching Baltim, Damietta and Port Said. Mubarak ordered Nasr to intercept. The 16 MiG-21s already airborne attacked the approaching jets in an effort to break up their formations. Another 16 MiG-21s from Mansourah and eight from Tanta also took off. At 1538 hrs Egyptian radar reported a third wave of 16 or so Phantom IIs coming in low from Port Said. The remaining eight MiG-21s at Mansourah took off to intercept them, while eight MiG-21s left Abu Hammad to help. The resulting engagement put 62 MiG-21s against 120 Phantom IIs and Skyhawks.

At 1552 hrs Egyptian radar detected yet another wave of around 60 F-4s and A-4s coming in low from the same directions as before. Their mission was to hit targets missed by the second wave. Eight MiG-21s were launched against them by No 102 Air Brigade at Inshas. An air battle was raging over Dekernis village, and when the third Israeli wave approached, they found that the second one had been unable to reach its target and was retreating eastward. Meanwhile, some 20 MiGs had landed to refuel and were now climbing back into battle. This convinced the leader of the final Israeli wave that the attack had failed. He ordered his pilots to retreat. The Israelis left Egyptian airspace at 1608 hrs.

Nasr Mousa recalled;

'There were eight of us, and while climbing we saw Israeli Phantom IIs approaching to make their bombing run. I got one in my sights, but remembered the number one rule – secure your tail before attacking the enemy. I looked in my mirror and saw a Phantom II lining up on me. I made a sudden tight right-hand turn, which put me on his tail, and I shot him down with cannon fire. There were no parachutes.'

Ahmed Yousef el-Wakeel said;

'It was arranged within our air regiment at el-Mansourah air base that two squadrons were for interceptions and air defence while the third, based at Tanta, was to defend both bases. Our losses were nil until 14 October. I fired at a Phantom II with my cannon because he was so close I could not use my missiles. There were two parachutes. I never realised how many 'planes there were during the battle. I was shocked when I heard the number, and we all joked, "Traffic jams on the ground in Egypt and now in its airspace as well!"'

Ahmad Nasr pointed out that Egyptian MiGs were outnumbered two to one during the battle, yet they scored heavily.

'There was also chivalry during the fighting. One pilot, Lt Mohamed Adoub, shot down a Phantom II but his MiG was damaged because he was so close to the exploding enemy. The Israeli and Mohamed jumped very near to one another, and local farmers almost killed the F-4 pilot. However, Mohammed saved him, and the Israeli was taken to the hospital. He had a visitor the next day – Mohamed Adoub.'

No Egyptian aircraft were destroyed during the first phase of the battle, although six MiG-21s were lost by the time it was over, including two which ran out of fuel and a third destroyed by debris from an exploding F-4. Three were downed by the enemy and two Egyptian pilots were killed. Tel Aviv, however, claimed the destruction of 15 Egyptian aircraft, while the final EAF claim for all fronts was 24, plus two helicopters.

On 15 October – the war's tenth day – the Israelis gave up targeting major air bases, but there was still a substantial air battle over the northern

Delta. It started at 1210 hrs when an estimated 24 Phantom IIs and 24 Mirages were met by a similar number of MiG-21s. The EAF claimed to have driven off the assault for the loss of two MiGs, with seven Israeli aircraft claimed as shot down. Outside observers estimated Israeli losses at this stage at 14 F-4s, 29 A-4s, three Mirages, four Super Mysteres and 28 unidentified aircraft. EAF losses were put at 49 MiGs of various types, 17 helicopters and 12 unidentified aircraft. Meanwhile, the supporting Soviet and American airlifts continued, as they had the previous day.

The next day Egypt's situation worsened further, and some MiG-21s from the Southern Air Region were sent north to help. A handful of Warsaw Pact advisers also started flying air defence missions, including East German Col Otto Abel, who flew at least ten Combat Air Patrols.

Certain differences were painfully apparent to surviving Egyptian MiG-21 pilots, including Ahmad Wafai. 'Israeli performance in dogfights got better and better on 15 and 16 October', he reported. At the time this was thought to be due to the presence of American 'volunteers' flying for Israel, but the main reason was the IDF/AF's acquisition of the latest dogfighting missiles, which could be fired at much higher G-loads and were themselves very manoeuvrable. Israeli tactics also changed, with the abandonment of large formations in favour of smaller groups and greatly increased use of ECM. This offensive against the EAF was code-named *Sudden Tornado*, and was intended to wipe out the cream of its MiG-21 units in no less than 19 'bait and trap' operations.

The ground situation was also worsening. An Israeli thrust split the Egyptian Sinai bridgehead in two, allowing tanks and infantry across to the western side of the Canal though what became known as the Deversoir Gap. The EAF now had to throw its aircraft into a savage struggle to protect the air defence network, while Egyptian Army units around Cairo and in the Delta rushed to contain the Israelis' 'counter-bridgehead'.

By Day 12 most EAF efforts were focussed on the Deversoir Gap. The IAF again attacked the base at Abu Hammad (Qattamiyah) during the morning. In the late afternoon they also struck Port Said, claiming the destruction of four Egyptian aircraft. An unusual combat also took place when a Dornier Do 27 on a forward observation mission north of the Mitla Pass was intercepted by four cannon-armed MiG-21PFs. One made a single firing pass. The Do 27 was hit twice, but the shells did not explode. With fuel tanks punctured, its pilot ordered his crew to bale out, set the aircraft on autopilot flying westwards, and baled out himself.

Aerial victory and loss claims now became unreliable, although the Egyptians' were the more inaccurate. At 1900 hrs Cairo reported there had been air battles almost all day, and that four Israeli aircraft had been shot down in combat for the loss of just one Egyptian jet. For their part, the Israelis claimed five EAF aircraft destroyed.

Air fighting over the Deversoir Gap remained intense the following day. Three major EAF attacks on Israeli bridges over the Suez Canal

This Israeli F-4E was hit by an R-3 'Atoll' missile fired from an Egyptian MiG-21MF and then finished off by 23 mm gunfire on 18 October 1973 (*Egyptian MoD via Tom Cooper*)

On 17 October 1973, this IDF/AF Dornier Do 27 was intercepted by EAF MiG-21s north of the Mitla Pass and shot up by cannon fire from one of the Egyptian fighters. The crew bailed out, leaving the unoccupied aircraft to continue flying westwards for 24 minutes before coming down near Cairo (*Tom Cooper collection*)

Kadri el-Hamid was Egypt's highest scoring MiG-21 fighter ace. He is seen here in 1976 during an advanced training course held in the USA. He ended his career with three F-4 Phantom IIs confirmed shot down and a Mirage shared with his wingman, Ahmad el-Assy, plus other aircraft damaged (*El-Hamid*)

This remarkable sequence of MiG-21 gun-camera photographs showing an Israeli Mirage exploding in flames was widely distributed by the Egyptian media after the October 1973 War. It is now known to have been taken by Dia el-Hefnawy during his combat on the 20th, the war's 15th day. The IDF/AF listed the loss of Nesher 9031, flown by Michael Katz, on this date, although he was reportedly brought down by AAA. Katz ejected from his blazing fighter (*EAF*)

achieved some success, although at a high cost in aircraft and helicopters. Tamim Fahmi Abd Allah summed up the difficulties facing the Egyptians during this final phase of the war;

'Look at the situation when the Israelis crossed the canal and took the missile line with their infantry and tanks. We were really at a disadvantage – we knew this – so we could only respond with aircraft which made it an air battle. We could only attack with a limited number of aircraft at one time, and they were waiting for us.'

Later in the day Israeli aircraft attacked Salihiyah air base again, and they ended the day claiming no less than 19 Egyptian aircraft destroyed in aerial combat. The Israelis also claimed to have shot down two North Korean-flown MiG-21s. Egyptian sources say the North Koreans, who were defending Egyptian rear areas, clashed with the Israelis twice and suffered no losses, but also claimed no victories. Meanwhile, the recently-arrived Soviet MiG-25s awaited an Israeli attack on Cairo West, where they were housed in underground shelters. The attack never came.

Day 14 saw more intensive fighting over the rapidly-expanding Israeli bridgehead. MiG-21s were committed to the ground-attack role, and Moustafa Hafiz was downed while attacking the bridges over the Gap. He was hit by a SAM, possibly a shoulder-launched MIM-43A Redeye. The MiGs attacked in sections of four at one-minute intervals. Hafiz recalled;

'The area was swarming with Israeli Mirages. I told my numbers two, three and four to make only one attack. It was impossible to make multiple passes. My wingman didn't acknowledge the message, so I went in, released my bombs and called him again. He said that he had not dropped his bombs, so I decided that we had to make another attack. At the initial point I saw a MiG-21 followed by three Mirages. I decided to support this MiG. Then I was hit in the right wing and started to roll to the left. That was when I ejected.'

Cairo claimed that four Israeli aircraft were downed by air defences in the morning, with another three being shot down in a big air battle in the afternoon. In contrast, the Israelis claim to have destroyed 25 aircraft, including 14 in battles west of the Canal – 11 of which supposedly fell during a single dogfight which ended at around 1700 hrs. Meanwhile, the Soviet airlift continued to replace EAF losses, although not pilots. Fortunately, most who ejected came down in Egyptian-held territory.

The struggle around and over the Gap continued on Day 15, with the Egyptians making their first serious counter-attack against the Israeli bridgehead. But it failed because Egyptian troops were now hopelessly exposed to attacks from Israeli fighter-bombers. Although the war was drawing to a close by 21 October (the 16th day) the aerial clashes grew even fiercer.

Despite his injured back, Kadri el-Hamid claimed the destruction of a Phantom II using his MiG-21's 23 mm cannon. Nabil Shoukry, CO of No 102 Air Brigade, based at Inshas, seems to have taken part in the same combat;

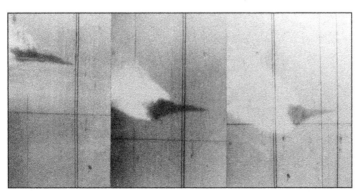

The ferocity of the air battles over the Suez Canal in the final days of the October 1973 War was regularly witnessed by international war correspondents and photographers, and here one of the latter has captured an Egyptian MiG-21MF, streaming fuel, in its final moments over Sinai. Although flown by highly-trained pilots, Arab MiG-21s remained weakly armed, and their ECM equipment was considerably inferior to that of their Israeli opponents (*Tom Cooper collection*)

Despite the damage inflicted to the tail-fin of this Egyptian MiG-21F-13 or MiG-21PF in combat on 29 October 1973, its pilot was still able to land safely (*EAF*)

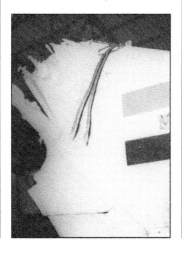

'In the final fights over Deversoir, we ambushed some Mirages by popping up from below, and my own "finger four" shot down four Mirages with the loss of one MiG.'

Dia el-Hefnawy took part in another combat further north, and the gun-camera film of the Mirage he shot down was widely distributed to the world's news media.

No specific information has emerged concerning Day 17 (22 October), Cairo claiming 12 Israeli aircraft downed, while Tel Aviv said 11 Egyptian aircraft had been destroyed. The following day Ahmed Atef was involved in one of the last big aerial battles of the war, and he was shot down after his engine failed. The Israeli Army attempted to reach the Red Sea south of Suez on 24 October, thus encircling the Egyptian Third Army. EAF aircraft attacked in large groups of up to 30 aircraft perhaps in the hope of swamping local Israeli air defences. This resulted in severe Egyptians casualties, as Farid Harfush confirmed;

'We lost a lot that day. We were obliged to do everything to protect the Third Army. It was like the Indians surrounding the wagons, and the whole Israeli Air Force were all over the Third Army.'

On the 25th a cease-fire supposedly came into effect on the Egyptian front, but clashes continued above the Egyptian Third Army throughout the subsequent armistice negotiations as the IDF/AF unsuccessfully tried to bomb the encircled Egyptians into submission.

The claim that Egypt was at Israel's mercy at the end of the war is incorrect. The Egyptians had largely re-established their SAM and anti-aircraft artillery defences, while on the ground, the military situation was relatively evenly balanced. In the air, however, there was no longer a balance. The Israelis had suffered massive losses, but had been re-supplied by the USA. They also had significant numbers of non-Israeli or dual-nationality 'volunteer' pilots within their ranks. The EAF had suffered even greater losses, and the USSR re-supplied a great deal via its 'air bridge'. But unlike the Israelis, the Egyptians could not find immediate replacements for lost or injured pilots.

The biggest air battles had been over the northern part of the Nile Delta, where a series of massive air attacks had been aimed at destroying EAF bases. There were four Israeli attacks on Tanta, four on Mansourah, three on Salihiyah, one on Quwaysina, four or five on Abu Hammad (sometimes referred to as Zaqaziq or Qattamiyah), one on Beni Sueif, one on Wadi Abu Rishah (Bir Arayida) and two on Abu Suweir, excluding probable smaller raids. Only two of these strikes were effective and the damage caused was repaired within a few hours. Furthermore, no Egyptian aircraft were destroyed on the ground.

In the air, it was clear that the Israelis still enjoyed a clear advantage, with more sophisticated and powerful equipment and superior training. In return, the EAF relied on what might be called the 'human factor', Egyptian pilots showing both dash and determination.

AMERIT AL-TAYARAN – THE RAMADAN WAR 1973

By the late summer of 1973, the SyAAF boasted ten MiG-21 squadrons equipped with over 100 operational aircraft, of which only 60 to 70 per cent were combat-ready. The number of MiG-21MFs was still very low, so older MiG-21F-13s and PFs were retained in service. Some MiG-21 units also had MiG-17s available for combat if necessary. From 1973, the SyAAF did not allow pilots below the rank of captain to fly fast jets. This policy, introduced to avoid inexperienced pilots having to face highly capable Israeli opponents in air combat, remains in force.

For SyAAF MiG-21-units, the October, or Ramadan, War started when eight 54th Sqn aircraft escorted 12 Su-20s on an attack against the IDF/AF control centre at Khevron at 1355 hrs. Minutes later, six 8th Sqn MiG-21MFs escorted 20 Su-7BMKs and 16 MiG-17s sent to bomb three Israeli radar sites at different points on the Golan Heights. Three flights of four MiG-21s each escorted three groups of eight to ten MiG-17s in attacks on Israeli Army strong points on the Golan. One MiG-17 was hit by radar-guided Bofors L70/40 flak and crashed in Lebanese territory. It was to be the first fighter shot down during the October 1973 War. Two minutes later, another group of MiG-21s escorted MiG-17s and Su-7s which hit Israeli tank parks near al-Qunay tirah. For the escorting MiG-21s, these first missions were relatively simple as Israeli fighters were not yet airborne.

But the second wave, comprising 30 Su-7s and MiG-17s, escorted by at least eight MiG-21s, clashed with Israeli jets. A MiG-21 crashed in Lebanon during a dogfight in which Capt Bassam Hamshu from the 5th Sqn downed an A-4 with a single 'Atoll' – the IDF/AF also lost a Mirage. Subsequently, the SyAAF was placed in strategic reserve while the SAM-belt along the Golan Heights front was activated. Beyond the front, a group of Syrian Mi-8 helicopters, covered by four MiG-21s, deployed commandos to capture an observation post on Mount Hermon.

The SyAAF flew approximately 270 sorties on 6 October, and by the end of the day the Syrians were in a fairly positive situation, enjoying command of the air over the front. Nevertheless, it was a race against time for both sides, and the Syrians had to attain their objectives before Israel mobilised its reserves.

This Syrian Air Force MiG-21F-13 was photographed undergoing maintenance in Czechoslovakia before delivery. The date of this shot is unknown, but it was probably taken before the October 1973 War (*authors' collections*)

NO LONGER MASTERS OF THE SKY

Late in the morning of 7 October the IDF/AF tried to strike Syrian SAM sites on the Golan so as to be able to operate freely over the battlefield. However, the Syrian Air Defence Force anticipated this reaction and prepared a trap, moving its sites to new positions overnight and leaving most under camouflage netting, rather than activating them at the first sign of Israeli fighters. Behind the front, pairs of MiG-21 waited for an opportunity to attack bomb-laden Israeli-fighters whose crews would be busy searching for ground targets.

At 1130 hrs the IDF/AF launched the first wave of 15 F-4Es, escorted by Neshers and some Mirage IIICs. Once over the Golan, the Phantom

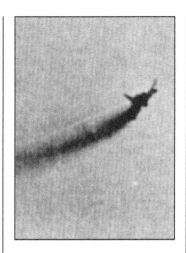

On the morning of 7 October, Syrian SAMs, anti-aircraft artillery and MiG-21 interceptors joined forces to claim seven F-4Es destroyed from a single Israeli squadron which attempted to attack air defence sites on the Golan front. This turned Operation *Dougman 5* into one of the costliest failures in IDF/AF history. Here, a damaged F-4E is seen trailing a column of smoke while trying to return to Israel. Seconds later it was shot down by R-3 missiles fired from Maj Kokach's MiG-21 (*Tom Cooper collection*)

II crews had considerable difficulty in finding their targets, so they spread out as they searched. At that moment the Syrian air defences opened fire, launching dozens of SAMs. As the F-4Es flew lower to evade the missiles they came into range of deadly radar-guided anti-aircraft guns. Five were shot down, and as the surviving Phantom IIs started to disengage, flying at very low altitude to avoid enemy fire, the MiGs appeared behind them.

The first section of 5th Sqn MiG-21MFs was led by Maj F Hegazi, with Capts M al-Zubair, M Badawi and H Shousha. Badawi was fastest, and caught a pair of F-4Es fleeing south-west at high speed. He fired all four of his missiles and one hit the rear jet, destroying an engine. Only then did the escorts react, a pair swooping behind two MiGs and downing both – Badawi and Hegazi ejected safely and were captured. Meanwhile, the crew of the damaged F-4 had to eject and, as so often, the Israelis recorded this as an 'operational loss', without specifying the reason.

Simultaneously, another pair of F-4Es was trying to escape the Syrian SAM-zone when one was damaged and started leaking fuel. Over Israeli lines, the limping Phantom II was bounced by two 5th Sqn MiG-21MFs, one of which was flown by Maj Kokach. Little more than a mile (two kilometres) behind them, the crews of two other Phantom IIs could see the MiGs manoeuvring behind the F-4s, and saw Maj Kokach launch a missile. The rear pair of Israelis downed Kokach's wingman with an AIM-9D. Meanwhile, Kokach's missile hit the F-4E, starting a fire in its left engine – the jet crashed seven miles (12 km) from an Israeli base. This time the Israelis attributed the loss to Syrian anti-aircraft fire.

The air offensive against Syrian air defences was an utter failure, with the IDF/AF losing control over the Golan. But the battle was not over, and both sides would suffer further losses.

Although it is widely believed that after the war's first day the SyAAF seldom operated over the Golan, the truth is very different. It continued sending MiG-21s on CAPs over the front, while others escorted strikes which caused severe losses to Israeli positions. Most packages comprised six to twelve ground-attack aircraft, escorted by four to eight MiG-21s. Except for their top cover, the Syrians flew in such tight formations that Israeli radars could not accurately assess their number. Sometimes such tactics even resulted in Israeli pilots failing to detect Syrian interceptors.

During the afternoon of 7 October, two sections of MiG-21s from al-Nasiriyah escorted a large group of Su-7s over the Golan. Guided by GCI, the first section, led by Capt Sarkees, followed the Sukhois flying at an altitude of 6500 ft (2000 m). Several kilometres behind was a second section of four MiG-21s.

Shortly before reaching the target area, Sarkees noticed two Israeli Mirages passing to his left at a distance of a mile (two kilometres), and at the same altitude, but flying in the opposite direction. Apparently not noticing the Syrians, these Mirages flew on and Sarkees, without using his radio to inform the rest of his formation, initiated a high-G turn and rolled out behind the Mirages. He closed swiftly and fired a single R-13M at the rear aircraft. It flew straight up the tailpipe, blowing the Mirage apart. There was no sign of an ejection – the Israelis reported that Ami Lahav was killed when his jet was lost to 'Syrian AAA'. Turning around, Sarkees was unable to locate the rest of his formation and so returned to base (*text continues on page 65*).

COLOUR PLATES

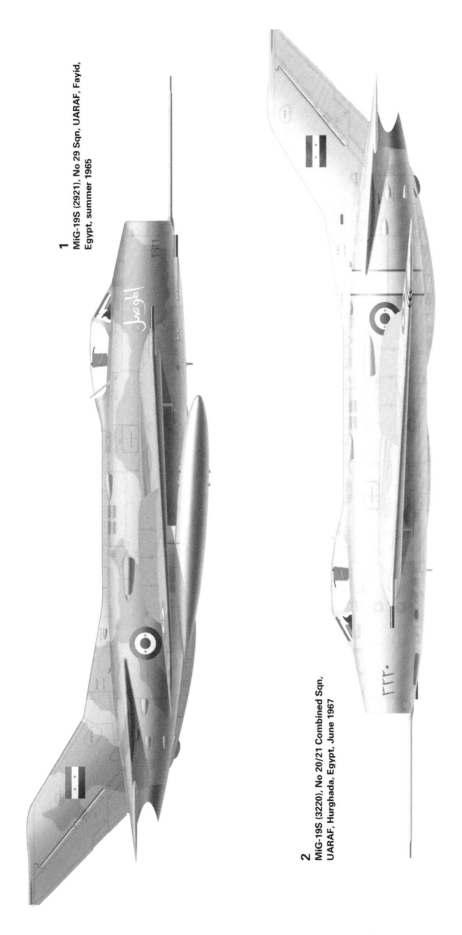

1
MiG-19S (2921), No 29 Sqn, UARAF, Fayid,
Egypt, summer 1965

2
MiG-19S (3220), No 20/21 Combined Sqn,
UARAF, Hurghada, Egypt, June 1967

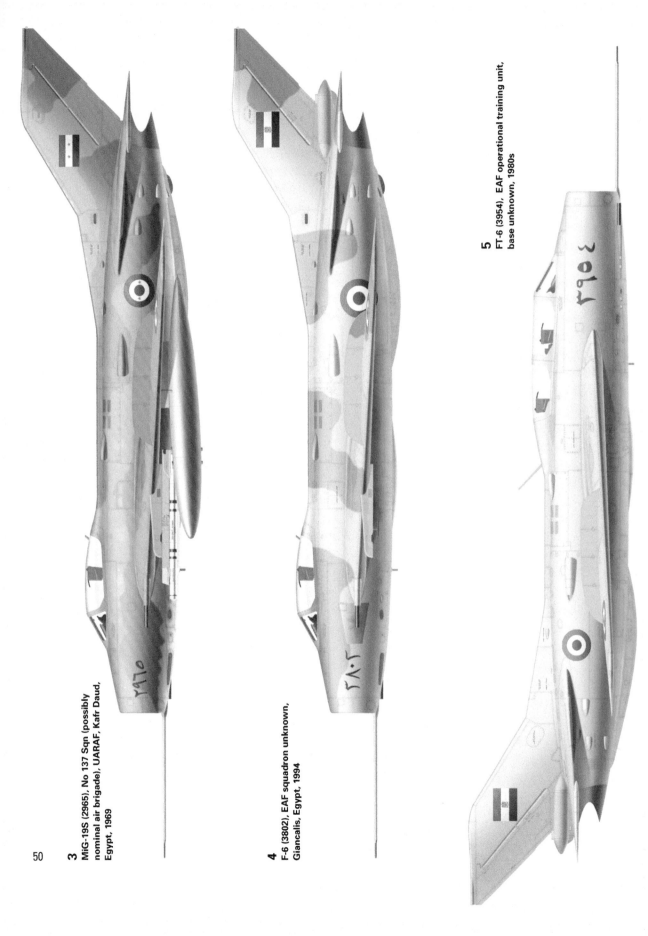

3
MiG-19S (2965), No 137 Sqn (possibly
nominal air brigade), UARAF, Kafr Daud,
Egypt, 1969

4
F-6 (3802), EAF squadron unknown,
Giancalis, Egypt, 1994

5
FT-6 (3954), EAF operational training unit,
base unknown, 1980s

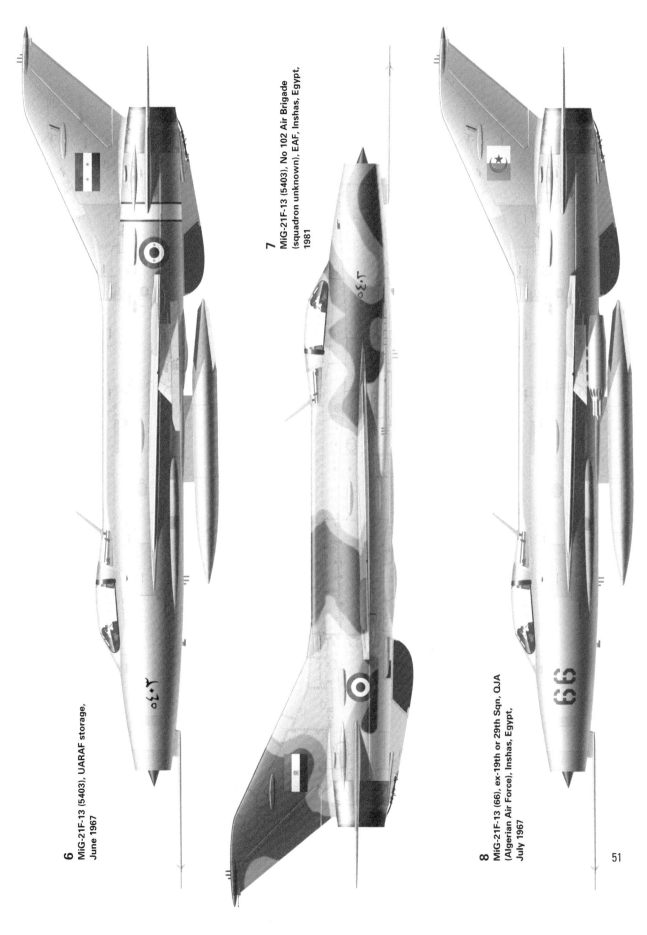

6
MiG-21F-13 (5403), UARAF storage,
June 1967

7
MiG-21F-13 (5403), No 102 Air Brigade
(squadron unknown), EAF, Inshas, Egypt,
1981

8
MiG-21F-13 (66), ex-19th or 29th Sqn, QJA
(Algerian Air Force), Inshas, Egypt,
July 1967

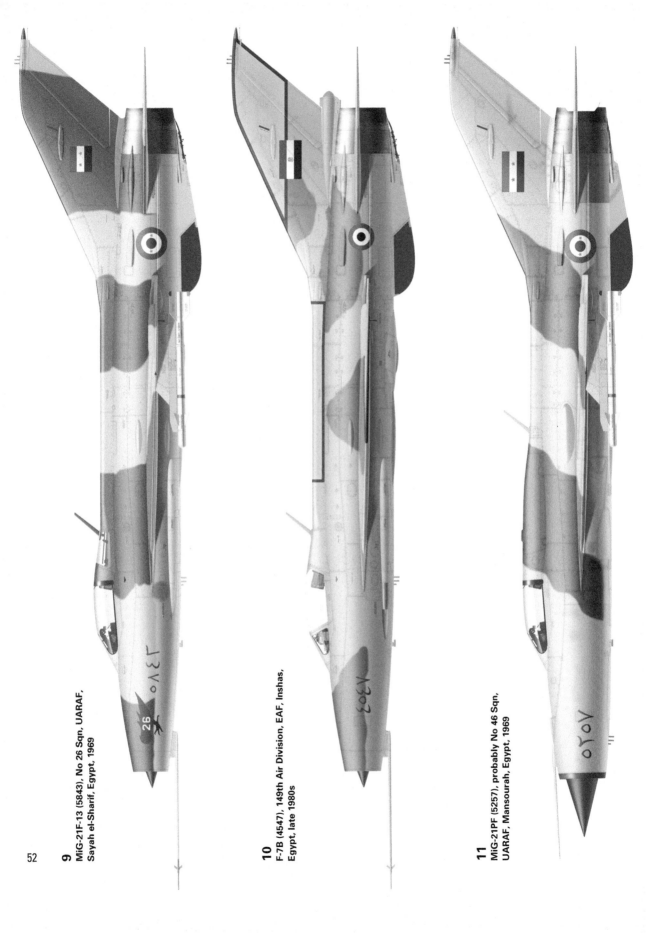

52

9
MiG-21F-13 (5843), No 26 Sqn, UARAF,
Sayah el-Sharif, Egypt, 1969

10
F-7B (4547), 149th Air Division, EAF, Inshas,
Egypt, late 1980s

11
MiG-21PF (5257), probably No 46 Sqn,
UARAF, Mansourah, Egypt, 1969

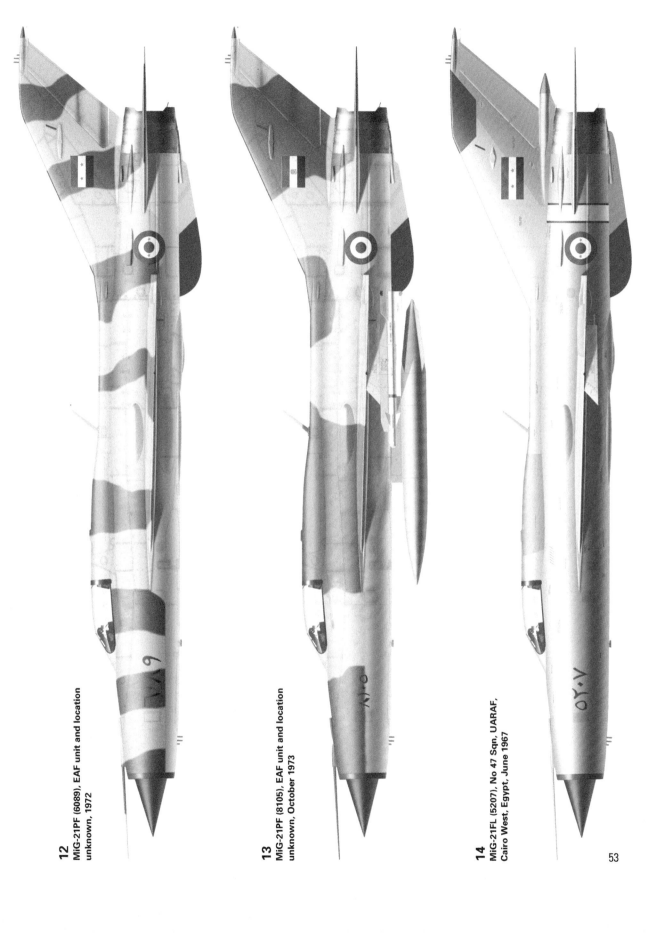

12
MiG–21PF (6089), EAF unit and location
unknown, 1972

13
MiG–21PF (8105), EAF unit and location
unknown, October 1973

14
MiG–21FL (5207), No 47 Sqn, UARAF,
Cairo West, Egypt, June 1967

53

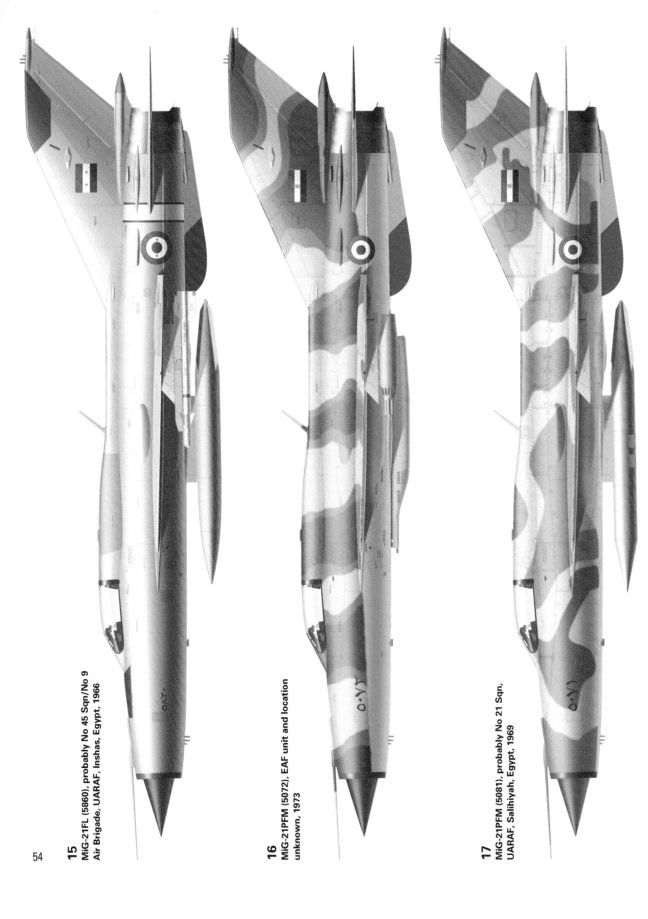

15
MiG-21FL (5860), probably No 45 Sqn/No 9
Air Brigade, UARAF, Inshas, Egypt, 1966

16
MiG-21PFM (5072), EAF unit and location
unknown, 1973

17
MiG-21PFM (5081), probably No 21 Sqn,
UARAF, Salihiyah, Egypt, 1969

54

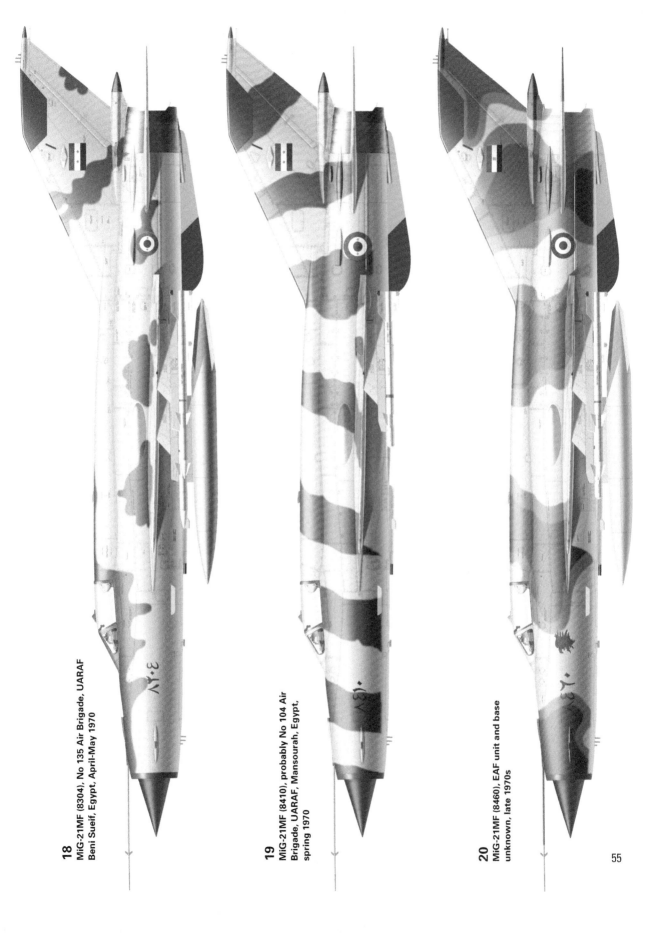

18
MiG-21MF (8304), No 135 Air Brigade, UARAF
Beni Sueif, Egypt, April-May 1970

19
MiG-21MF (8410), probably No 104 Air
Brigade, UARAF, Mansourah, Egypt,
spring 1970

20
MiG-21MF (8460), EAF unit and base
unknown, late 1970s

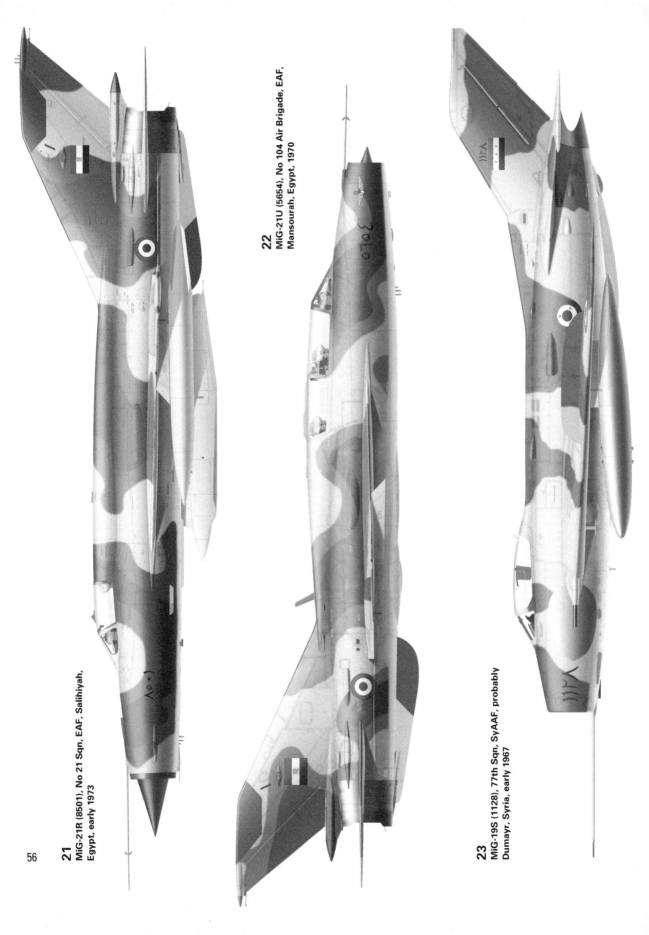

21
MiG-21R (8501), No 21 Sqn, EAF, Salihiyah,
Egypt, early 1973

22
MiG-21U (5654), No 104 Air Brigade, EAF,
Mansourah, Egypt, 1970

23
MiG-19S (1128), 77th Sqn, SyAAF, probably
Dumayr, Syria, early 1967

56

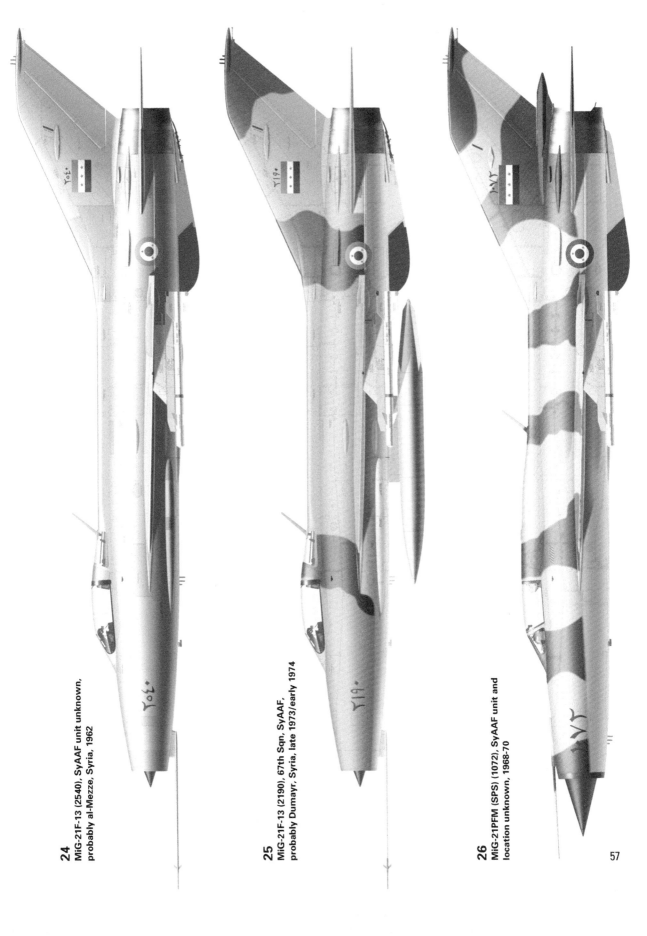

24
MiG-21F-13 (2540), SyAAF unit unknown,
probably al-Mezze, Syria, 1962

25
MiG-21F-13 (2190), 67th Sqn, SyAAF,
probably Dumayr, Syria, late 1973/early 1974

26
MiG-21PFM (SPS) (1072), SyAAF unit and
location unknown, 1968-70

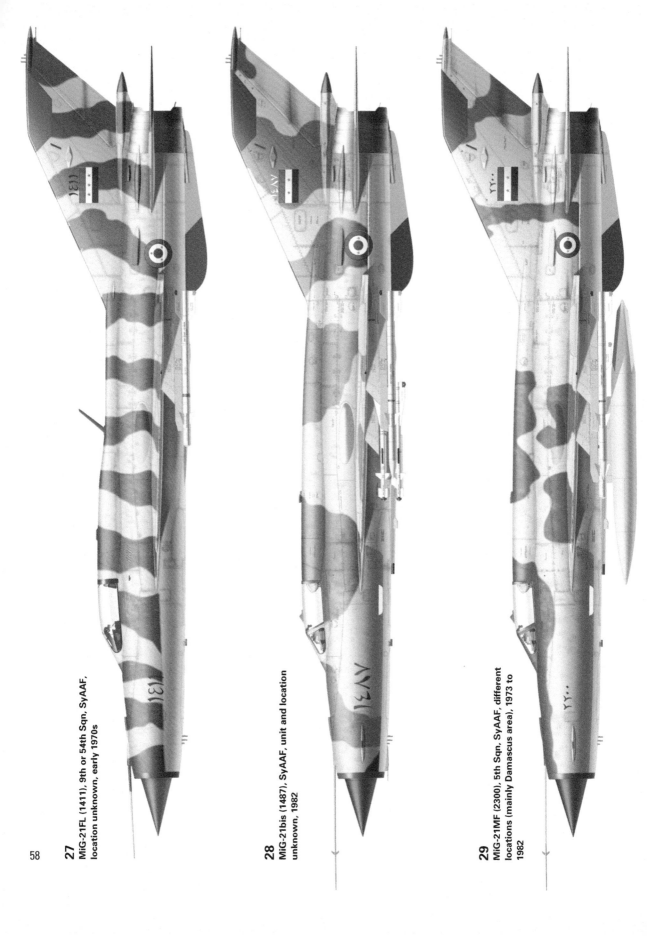

58

27
MiG-21FL (1411), 9th or 54th Sqn, SyAAF,
location unknown, early 1970s

28
MiG-21bis (1487), SyAAF, unit and location
unknown, 1982

29
MiG-21MF (2300), 5th Sqn, SyAAF, different
locations (mainly Damascus area), 1973 to
1982

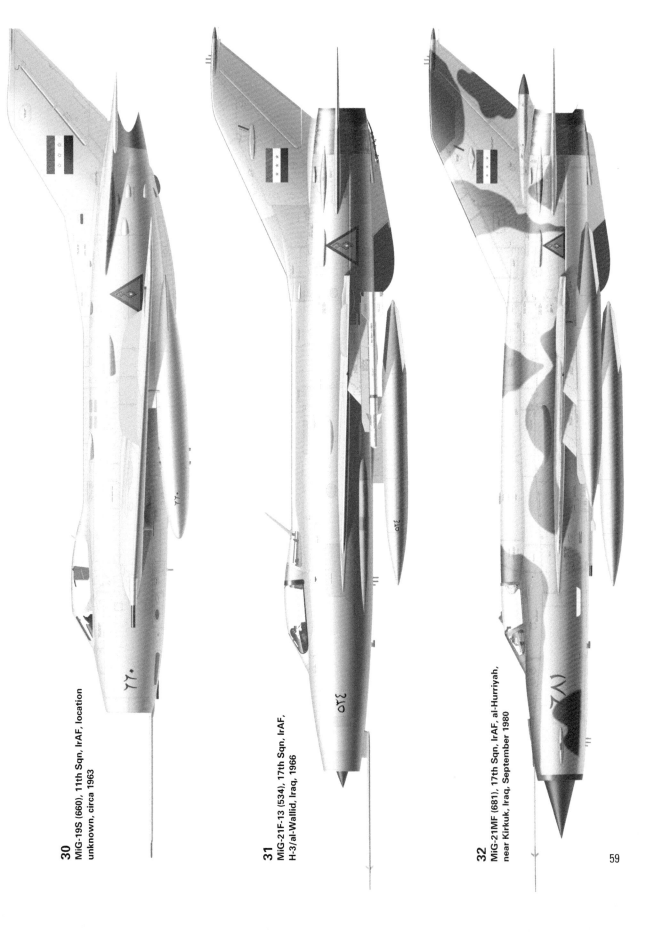

30
MiG-19S (660), 11th Sqn, IrAF, location
unknown, circa 1963

31
MiG-21F-13 (534), 17th Sqn, IrAF,
H-3/al-Wallid, Iraq, 1966

32
MiG-21MF (681), 17th Sqn, IrAF, al-Hurriyah,
near Kirkuk, Iraq, September 1980

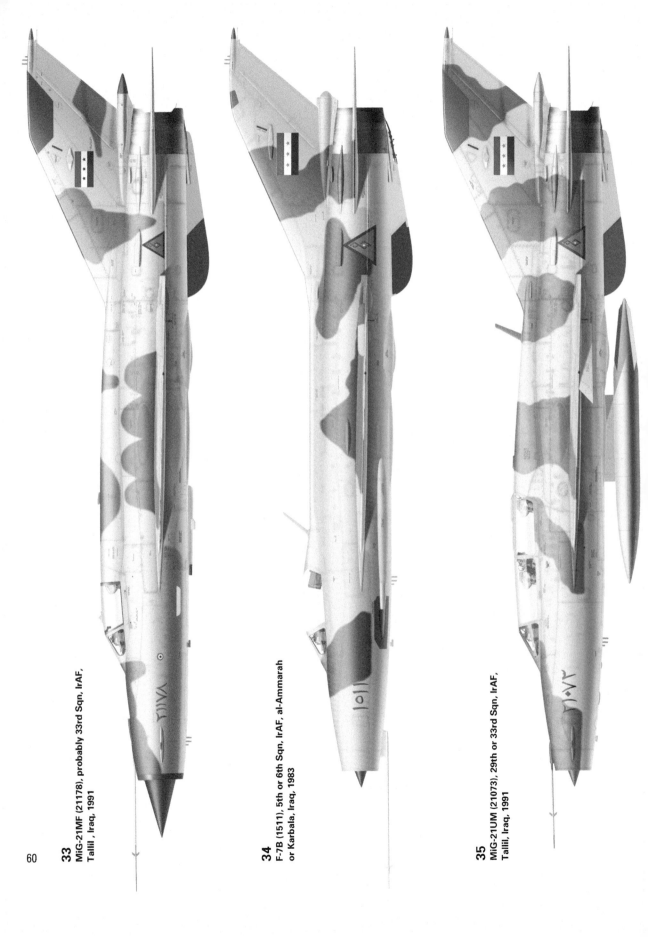

33
MiG-21MF (21178), probably 33rd Sqn, IrAF,
Tallil , Iraq, 1991

34
F-7B (1511), 5th or 6th Sqn, IrAF, al-Ammarah
or Karbala, Iraq, 1983

35
MiG-21UM (21073), 29th or 33rd Sqn, IrAF,
Tallil, Iraq, 1991

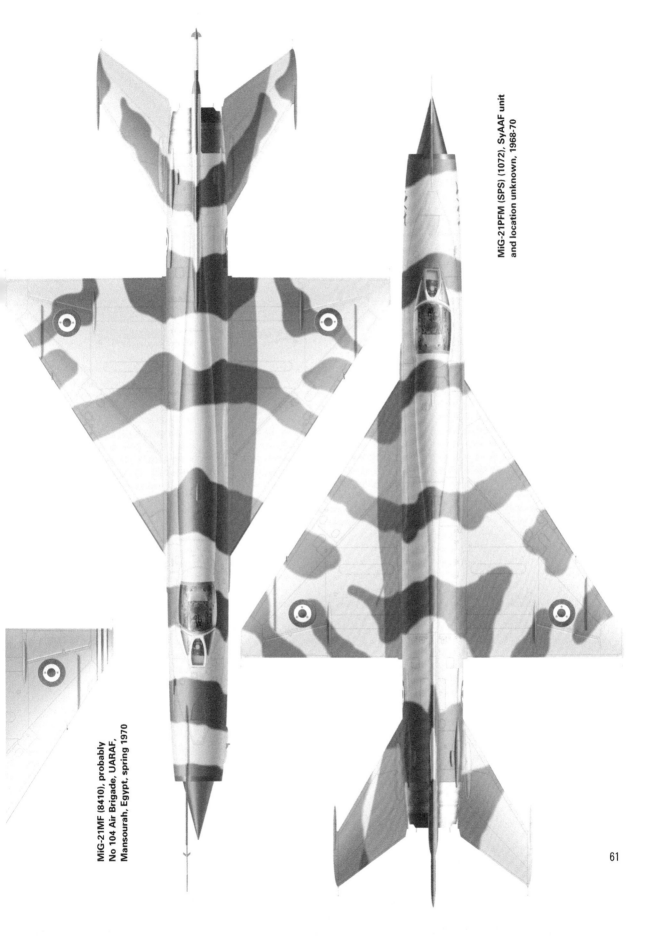

MiG-21PFM (SPS) (1072), SyAAF unit
and location unknown, 1968-70

MiG-21MF (8410), probably
No 104 Air Brigade, UARAF,
Mansourah, Egypt, spring 1970

61

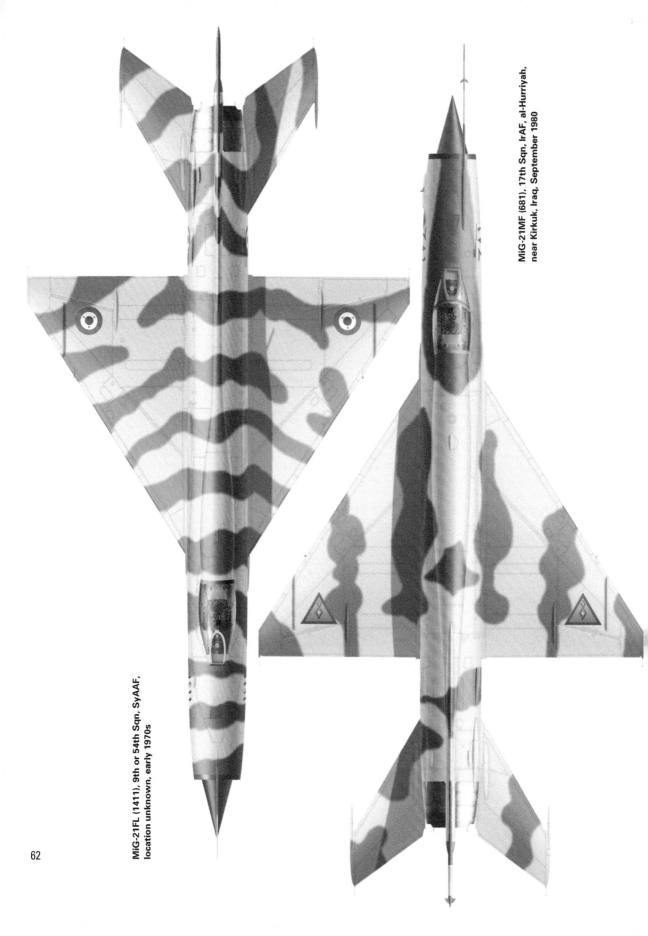

MiG-21FL (1411), 9th or 54th Sqn, SyAAF,
location unknown, early 1970s

MiG-21MF (681), 17th Sqn, IrAF, al-Hurriyah,
near Kirkuk, Iraq, September 1980

1

2

3

4

5

6

Meanwhile, Capt Dauvara, leader of the rear pair of MiG-21s, detected two more Mirages some 30 degrees to his left. Again, the Israeli pilots failed to notice their enemies. This time Dauvara ordered a hard turn and rolled out, followed by his wingman, Capt Dibbs, some 2000 ft (600 m) behind the rear Mirage. Dauvara got a lock-on and pressed the trigger, but because he fired from inside the minimal envelope the 'Atoll' passed the target without exploding. But Dibbs attacked the Israeli leader from 2600 ft (800 m) and fired another missile which exploded inside the enemy's tailpipe. The rear Mirage, still pursued by Dauvara, initiated a tight spiral towards the ground and escaped southward. With no other targets in sight, Dauvara and Dibbs returned to base.

The second section of MiG-21s now appeared over the target area at 10,000 ft (3000 m) and clashed with four Mirages. Dividing into two pairs, the Syrian pilots engaged the Israelis for so long that only one Su-7 was shot down after a wild pursuit between the hills of the northern Golan. Some additional air-to-air missiles were fired but no further hits were achieved, after which both sides disengaged. Due to their very low fuel, status all four pilots decided to land at 'Bley', probably meaning the Qabr al-Sitt Highway Strip near the village of Mlayha. But the local air defence units failed to recognise them and three MiG-21s were shot down by 'friendly fire'. One pilot was killed.

Elsewhere that day, Capt Bassam Hamshu led a section of four 5th Sqn MiG-21MFs to intercept Phantom IIs and Skyhawks approaching over Lebanon, escorted by Mirages. A fierce combat broke out as the opposing formations met at low level. Hamshu downed a Skyhawk and a Mirage, with his twin 23 mm GSh-23 guns, while one of his wingmen claimed a Phantom II. Two MiG-21MFs were also lost. In total, the SyAAF flew 210 sorties on 7 October and claimed to have shot down 12 Israeli aircraft for the loss of 14 of their own.

That same day an IrAF contingent, led by Col Yasir Abdullah, with Capt H R Sholah as his deputy, entered the war. It comprised 20 Hunters and 18 Su-7BMKs, with 18 MiG-21PFs of the 9th Sqn. All were based at al-Mezzeh. The Iraqis also brought 11 contract pilots with them from Russia, East Germany, Poland, Libya and Britain. But the Iraqi involvement did not get off to a very good start. An Su-7BMK and a MiG-21PF were shot down by Israeli Mirages on their first strike. In return, the Iraqi MiG-21s claimed two Skyhawks.

The struggle intensified on 8 October when the IDF/AF tried to stem the Syrian armoured onslaught on the Golan Heights, while also making its first major strikes against Syrian airfields. This resulted in the highest losses suffered by the IDF/AF in a single day when at least 23 aircraft were shot down. Another

The Syrian Air Force remains one of the most secretive in the world, and even today very few photographs of its aircraft have been released. Those which have, like this one of a MiG-21MF taken during the first half of the 1970s, tend to be of very poor quality (*SyAAF*)

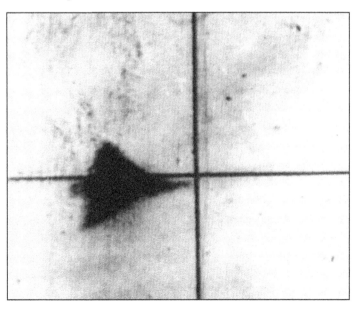

The SyAAF is not known to have officially released any gun-camera pictures, as they are considered to be military secrets, but this is an exception. It shows the Israeli Mirage IIIC (flown by Ami Lahav, who was killed) shot down by Capt Bassam Hamshu on 7 October 1973. The IDF/AF claimed that the jet was brought down by AAA (*Tom Cooper collection*)

30 returned to their bases badly damaged, most having been hit over Syria. The Israelis now tried to fly around the Syrian SAM belt by going north over Lebanon or south over Jordan. They flew low along valleys and escarpments, then turned towards Damascus or attacked Syrian ground forces from the east. This made detection and tracking difficult for the Syrians, but it gave them greater reaction time.

Early in the morning, at around 0700 hrs, a section of MiG-21s led by Capt al-Hamidi bounced four Phantom IIs which were attacking Dmeyr air base. Closing to about 4000 ft (1300 m), al-Hamidi fired his first missile, but it flew straight ahead and was never under guidance. Accelerating, the Syrian pilot had approached to 3000 ft (900 m) when the F-4 pilots suddenly initiated a break. Nevertheless, al-Hamidi's second missile found its mark and damaged a Phantom II, which subsequently crashed. The pilot was killed, but the WSO ejected and was captured.

Minutes later, a 7th Sqn section led by Capt Asaf surprised four F-4s in the Tartus area. All the Syrian pilots managed to fire their missiles, but they either malfunctioned or were launched too close, as only one of Asaf's scored a hit. A Phantom II immediately fell, while the rest of the Israeli formation accelerated and outpaced the MiGs westward.

Almost two hours later another F-4 formation was detected approaching Sayqal air base. Eight MiG-21s led by Capt Kahwaji were scrambled, and the two formations clashed head-to-head north of Damascus. A wild mêlée followed in which Kahwaji outmanoeuvred one of the Phantom IIs and attacked it with two missiles. One went ballistic but the other scored a direct hit, entering the F-4E's jet-pipe and reducing the aircraft to a brilliant fireball. Kahwaji's aircraft was then hit by another Phantom II, but he ejected safely. Meanwhile, Capt Jelyi got behind an F-4 and fired both his missiles, one exploding under the target. A large trail of fire and smoke appeared and the jet subsequently crashed. Short of fuel, Jelyi tried to land at al-Nasiriyah, but the base was already under Israeli attack and his MiG was hit by a Syrian SA-6. He was killed instantly.

The Iraqi MiG-21s were less successful that day. Four MiGs, escorting a large formation of Hunters, were unable to help when the Israeli Hawk SAMs and Mirages knocked down three of their charges over the Golan. Iraqi Su-7BMKs enjoyed better fortune the following morning when they hit Israeli armour around al-Qunaytirah. This time they were escorted by a quartet of Syrian MiG-21MFs, one of which was flown by Capt al-Zo'aby, who shot down an A-4E. This Syrian pilot has not previously been positively identified because the al-Zo'aby clan is one of the largest in southern Syria, and has a strong tradition of serving with the SyAAF.

Shortly after Zo'aby's engagement, the IDF/AF dispatched 16 F-4s, escorted by Mirages and Neshers, against the SyAAF headquarters in the prosperous Abu Rummanneh

The tail of an IDF/AF F-4E Phantom II of No 69 'Hammers' Sqn, shot down over the Golan front during the October 1973 War. The Syrians credited its demise to a MiG-21, although this cannot be confirmed. The wreckage was photographed among a huge pile of smashed Israeli aircraft in the Damascus Military Museum in August 1974 (*D Nicolle*)

On 10 October 1973 Capt Gallal Eddeen Khaddam surprised and shot down two Israeli Mirages within seconds of each other during an air battle over the Golan Heights. For this achievement he was decorated with the Hero of the Republic Medal, one of the highest Syrian military decorations (*Syrian National TV via Yasser al-Abed*)

district of Damascus. A total of 26 Syrian civilians were killed and 117 injured – a toll which increased Syrian determination to fight.

Later that day dozens of engagements erupted over the Golan Heights and inside Syria, during which the SyAAF claimed six Israeli aircraft shot down. These claims included two Phantom IIs destroyed by Capt Adeeb el-Gar during a battle over Homs. In another engagement, two MiG-21MFs of the 5th Sqn, led by Capt Bassam Hamshu, intercepted an Israeli RF-4E over the Golan. Hamshu used three of his four R-13M missiles to hit the jet, but moments later both he and his wingman were shot down by two F-4Es using Sidewinder missiles. Both Syrians ejected safely. Elsewhere, the MiG-21PFs of the Iraqi 9th Sqn were less successful, claiming an Israeli Super Mystere B2 for the loss of two of their own, plus two Hunters, all downed by Israeli Mirages.

THE ISRAELI ONSLAUGHT

On 10 October – the war's fifth day – came the largest clashes over the Golan Heights so far, with both the SyAAF and the IDF/AF throwing most of their serviceable aircraft into the fray. The Israelis later claimed no less than 19 Syrian aircraft downed, while the Syrians and Iraqis claimed to have shot down 16 Israeli jets in air combat alone. Whatever the true figures, there is no doubt that the Syrians began to feel increasing pressure from the better-trained and more experienced Israelis pilots. SAM units were also hampered by a missile shortage, and at one point they stopped firing SAMs altogether, throwing the brunt of responsibility for air defence onto the remaining MiG-21s.

Early in the morning, four MiG-21s, led by Capt al-Najjar, took-off from al-Nasiriyah. Arriving over Golan, the section split, with the leading pair at 13,000 ft (4000 m) and the rear pair further back at 19,500 ft (6000 m). After several minutes, the leader of the second pair, Capt Gallal Eddeen Khaddam, spotted four Mirages closing at 10,000 ft (3000 m). Khaddam alerted his leader and started an attack, rolling out about 2600 ft (800 m) behind a pair of Israeli fighters. Working quickly, Khaddam locked onto the first opponent and fired two missiles within seconds of each other, aimed at the Israeli wingman and leader. To his surprise, both missiles guided properly and scored hits. One Mirage blew up and the other fell in flames. Subsequently, two other pilots from this Syrian formation claimed victories against Mirages or Neshers, but after the war only Khaddam was decorated with the Hero of the Republic Medal for this combat.

The IDF/AF opened a massive onslaught the next morning, targeting Syrian airfields, power installations, harbour facilities and other important sites across the country. Weakened by losses, the SyAAF pulled many mothballed MiG-17s and MiG-21s out of reserve and flew constant air patrols, initiating a number of engagements. At Sayqal, however, eight MiGs were surprised by a flight of F-4s and were destroyed on the ground, although one Iraqi MiG-21 pilot claimed to have shot down a Phantom II.

Over the front, other massive engagements developed, some of them involving between 30 and 60 aircraft. These were fought at altitudes of between 160 ft (50 m) and 20,000 ft (6000 m), and at speeds varying from 125 to 900 mph (200 and 1500 km/h). Many missiles were fired.

Syrian and Iraqi MiG-21 pilots alike were hampered by poor visibility from their cockpits and unreliable missiles. Nor could they make effective use of advantages such as the MiG-21's small silhouette. Even its turning performance was little help when attacks could come at any moment from any side. Inevitably, many losses were suffered, and in one battle a SyAAF brigade stationed at Dumayr lost eight MiG-21s. Only Capt Hamshu remained successful, downing his third A-4, again by gunfire. Another Skyhawk was shot down by Iraqi 9th Sqn MiG-21s, which were escorting an attack mission by Iraqi Hunters, although two of the latter were lost.

Conditions had worsened by 12 October. The IDF/AF stepped up its strikes, while an Iraqi division moving towards the front was ambushed and severely battered. Nevertheless, that morning the 5th Sqn scrambled four MiG-21MFs to intercept Israeli Phantom IIs over Sasa. The Syrians succeeded in surprising the Israeli crews, firing six missiles and downing an F-4E. In the afternoon, Maj Fayez Mansour claimed a Mirage during a brief dogfight over the Golan. His victim was Capt Ami Roke'ach, who was captured. Mansour was subsequently decorated for shooting down one F-4E and two Mirages between October 1973 and the end of the fighting in early 1974.

The next 'confrontation' took place in Damascus. After the heavy losses suffered by the Iraqi ground forces, which had been hit from the ground and from the air due to a lack of air support, Iraqi officers Col Abdullah and Capt Sholah went to SyAAF HQ. There, they accused the air force's commander, Gen Jamil, and Col Ali Saleh, CO of the air defence forces, of failing to provide air support for Iraqi ground units. As a result of these accusations, the Syrians had to admit the full truth about their losses. The Iraqi commander and his staff were shocked by the number of aircraft lost, but were also furious that the Syrians had concealed this, and other information.

Abdullah was then recalled, and in his place the IrAF sent Gen Qasim Masri to al-Mezzeh on 13 October, together with 11 brand-new MiG-21MFs from the 17th Sqn. Their pilots had just finished conversion training, undertaken with the help of Indian Air Force instructors. Without a proper understanding of what was actually going on at the front, Masri ordered this Iraqi contingent to 'destroy the IDF/AF'!

Meanwhile, the SyAAF was reorganising. On 11 October the remaining four 12th Sqn MiG-21PFs had been sent from al-Suwaydah to Marj Ruhayyil, where they came under the control of the 8th Squadron, which itself had only three or four MiG-21s intact. The following day the remaining two 11th Sqn MiG-21MFs joined them from Khalkhalah. Meanwhile, four battle-damaged MiG-21F-13s and two MiG-21PFs were assembled at Jirah. With the help of six Pakistani and several SyAAF instructors, one or two of them were repaired and returned to service on 13 October.

Despite the arrival of the new IrAF unit, Iraqi-Syrian tension peaked as the IrAF tried to organise an operation in support of Iraqi troops. That morning, an Iraqi Hunter FR 9 flown by British mercenary Robert Conner was shot down by Syrian SAMs while returning from a sortie over Mount Hermon. In fact, the Iraqis suffered heavier losses from Syrian air defences than from the Israelis, primarily because Syrian Air Defence

During the final days of the October 1973 War, fierce air battles developed around Mount Hermon, when both sides lost many aircraft. In the heat of battle the pilots would frequently drop down to very low levels, like this SyAAF MiG-21MF, armed with four R-3 missiles, photographed while over-flying Damascus at high speed (*Tom Cooper collection*)

Capt Adeeb el-Gar was one of the most successful Syrian MiG-21 fighter pilots, being credited with five confirmed F-4 Phantom IIs and one Nesher destroyed. All these successes were achieved between 13 September and 24 October 1973 (*Syrian National TV via Yasser al-Abed*)

units could not recognise their IFF systems as 'friendly'.

Conner's reconnaissance film was desperately needed, but now the Iraqis had to deliver their next strike without it. As a result, a large formation of Hunters and Su-7BMKs, escorted by 9th Sqn MiG-21PFs, flew into an Israeli trap. No less than four sections of Phantom IIs, Neshers and Mirages met them, shooting down one Hunter, two MiG-21s and three Su-7BMKs. In exchange, Iraqi MiG-21s claimed two Mirages and two Super Mystere B2s, although they seem to have damaged only one or two Israeli fighters. A second Iraqi effort, undertaken in the afternoon, was no more successful. Four MiG-21s from the 9th and 17th Sqns were shot down by Israeli F-4Es and Mirages over Mas'hara. Finally, an IrAF 9th Sqn MiG-21PF was shot down by Syrian Army anti-aircraft fire and its East German pilot, H Sluszkiewicz, killed.

The fact that Syrian Capt Bassam Hamshu claimed an Israeli Bell 205 helicopter destroyed on the ground – the Israeli pilot having landed when confronted by the MiG – did not help the Iraqis. The following morning, the IrAF ordered foreign personnel to leave Syria, while its remaining fighters were pulled back to Dumayr. Surviving Su-7BMKs, together with stocks of spares, were handed over to the Syrians, while the remaining Hunters returned to Iraq. Only the few MiG-21s of the 9th and 17th Sqns remained under Iraqi command inside Syria.

Paradoxically, Day 11 (16 October) of the war was one of the SyAAF's most successful. In the morning, four MiG-21s tried to intercept Phantoms II which were intending to bomb port facilities in Tartus, but clashed instead with a section of escorting Mirages. Despite being surprised by the enemy, Capt Asaf claimed a Mirage destroyed with missiles. Several hours later, a pair of MiG-21MFs from Hama, flown by Capt Adeeb el-Gar, and one of the pilots from the Zo'aby family, were on a CAP over Tartus when they noticed a solitary Phantom II about four miles (six kilometres) away.

The F-4E, which was obviously acting as bait, did a slow turn, inviting the MiGs to pursue. Both Syrians accelerated, jettisoned their drop tanks and engaged afterburner. The Israeli accelerated at low level, but the MiG-21MF could fly as fast as a Phantom II under such circumstances. El-Gar and Zo'aby were soon in position to fire missiles. The first was fired from a range of 4500 ft (1400 m), but to no effect. Three others either missed or the Israeli pilot evaded them. By closing to less than 2000 ft (600 m), el-Gar failed because he was too close to his target. Meanwhile, the situation had changed. Another F-4E appeared behind the Syrian pair and swiftly hit the MiG of Capt al-Zo'aby, forcing him to eject. Then el-Gar's engine stalled, but as he was still flying much faster than the Phantom II in front of him, he engaged his foe with his 23 mm guns.

In el-Gar's own words;

This photograph has been published several times, and is usually said to show a mortally-damaged Egyptian MiG-21 shot down by Israeli interceptors. In fact, it comes from a sequence of photographs taken on the Golan Heights on 24 October 1973, showing an Israeli F-4E Phantom II going down in flames after an air battle with Syrian MiG-21s. The aircraft crashed near a squadron of Israeli Centurion tanks, but the identity of the Syrian pilot who achieved this kill remains unknown (*Tom Cooper collection*)

'Even though the engine was not operating, I continued to close with the Phantom II because of excessive speed. I managed to fire four bursts from the cannon from ranges between 300 and 400 m (1000 and 1300 ft). I saw strikes in the wing root and then the F-4 caught fire and entered a slow right turn, before splashing into the sea. I restarted the engine at 1500 m (4900 ft).'

Barely 24 hours later, eight MiG-21s, led by Maj Kokach and Capt al-Ali, clashed with a group of Phantom IIs over the Golan Heights. Both Kokach and el-Ali claimed one kill, but the rest of their formation – six aircraft – was shot down and two pilots killed.

Over the following days, the IDF/AF was primarily engaged in supporting the Israeli ground offensive across the Suez Canal in Egypt. The Golan front remained relatively quiet as the Syrians brought in reinforcements, while Iraqi and Jordanian forces were beginning local counterattacks. In fact the Arabs were preparing for a large new offensive on this eastern front, planned for 24 October.

Meanwhile, the Israelis attempted to recapture their lost observation post on Mount Herman, prompting several air battles. On the 21st Capt al-Hamidi was flying alone over el-Mezze air base when it was attacked by several Phantom IIs. He went in pursuit of the fighter-bombers, but over the Golan Heights was attacked by at least two Israeli aircraft which fired three missiles at his MiG-21MF. Al-Hamidi evaded them all, reversed and counter-attacked, using the better turning performance of his MiG. Within seconds, he approached one of the Phantom IIs and downed it with 23 mm cannon. Al-Hamidi was then himself shot down by the second F-4E. He ejected over Israeli-held territory and was captured.

The next day Capt al-Taweel engaged four Neshers. After evading three missiles, he claimed a Nesher using an R-13M missile. The same day Capt Adeeb el-Gar also claimed a Nesher over an-Nasiriyah, although three more MiG-21s were shot down, their pilots ejecting safely.

The next air combat involving SyAAF MiG-21s erupted on 22 October when Capts al-Masry and al-Taweel from the 54th Sqn each claimed a Nesher destroyed over Mount Hermon. Further kills were claimed on the 23rd when four MiG-21s engaged four Mirages almost directly over Beirut. During this battle, Capt Shakruw stated that he shot down a Nesher using missiles. His formation disengaged without loss. Shortly afterwards, four MiG-21s clashed with four more Neshers over Mount Hermon, and Capt Habal claimed one of the Israeli fighters. During this dogfight two other MiG-21s were shot down, while Habal's aircraft was badly damaged by a missile which exploded close behind the fin. The pilot managed to land safely at Dumayr, where no less than 12 large holes were found in his aircraft.

CONTINUING TENSIONS

Despite the cease-fire, which supposedly brought the October War to a close, low-level fighting continued, and on 6 December 1973 there was a brief clash over Sukhna, south of Suez. The EAF claimed to have downed an Israeli F-4E, which the IDF/AF denied. The Israelis claimed a MiG-21, and this was also denied by the Egyptians.

The MiG-25s of the Soviet 154th SAG remained in Egypt, despite a serious deterioration in relations between the Egyptian and Soviet governments. They continued to fly reconnaissance over Israeli-occupied Sinai, protected on departure and return by Egyptian MiG-21s. The final mission was flown on 15 December, but the last Soviet military advisers did not leave Egypt until August 1974.

Inevitably, the collapse of relations between Egypt and the USSR caused problems for the EAF, which had to find alternative sources of equipment. The Egyptians, however, were already signalling their changed allegiance, which was even being reflected in the structure of the air force. By the autumn of 1974 a Southern Air District and four air divisions had formed another structural layer above the Soviet-style air brigades.

Two divisions were primarily concerned with air defence – the 139th at Mansourah and the 149th at Inshas. They incorporated air units in northern and central Egypt, and provided administrative and logistical control, while operational control remained in the hands of EAF headquarters in Cairo. The Southern Air District exercised operational control over aircraft within its area, but the main operational EAF element remained with the air brigades, which

An EAF MiG-21MF (probably from No 25 Sqn), serial number 8427, as it appeared in the late 1970s. It also wears the standard Soviet two-colour camouflage scheme applied before delivery to Egypt, but displays a version of the 'bat' motif of the UARAF's first nightfighter squadron before the Six Day War. Following Egypt's peace agreement with Israel, more EAF fighter squadrons started adding unit insignia to their aircraft (*EAF*)

Two EAF MiG-21MFs (serial numbers 8611 and 8652) make a low-level pass for the benefit of the camera. Both jets display versions of the Soviet-style two-colour camouflage, rather than any of the schemes normally applied in Egypt (*EAF*)

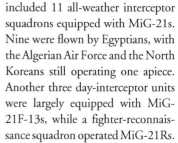

This EAF MiG-21PF, in its original markings and colour scheme, was put on display outside the October 1973 Panorama Museum in Cairo. Unfortunately, the aircraft has since been repainted in different, and largely inappropriate, colours (*Sherif Sharmy*)

included 11 all-weather interceptor squadrons equipped with MiG-21s. Nine were flown by Egyptians, with the Algerian Air Force and the North Koreans still operating one apiece. Another three day-interceptor units were largely equipped with MiG-21F-13s, while a fighter-reconnaissance squadron operated MiG-21Rs.

For a long time the USSR refused to return an estimated 140 MiG-21s sent to the Soviet Union for major refurbishment after the October 1973 War, and the EAF may still have had only 100 operational MiG-21s available at the time of its brief border war with Libya in 1977, although by then 50 jets had indeed been returned by the USSR.

Egyptian efforts to obtain new or at least replacement combat aircraft ran into considerable difficulty after the 1973 war. Even as late as 1975, Egypt was still negotiating by buy the third-generation MiG-21SMT, although nothing came of this. The peace agreement with Israel caused huge problems in Egypt's relations with most other Arab countries, although it did open up new sources of fighter aircraft which eventually included China, France, Great Britain, the USA and Italy. These varied sources of hardware, when added to the EAF's existing arsenal, led to some confusion, but the Egyptians coped well with such problems.

In 1977 No 224 Air Brigade changed from being a fighter-bomber unit with Su-7s to the reconnaissance role, equipped with elderly MiG-21Rs and new French-built Mirage 5Rs. The Egyptians also reportedly gave some of their most advanced MiG-21s to the USA as part of a deal to receive F-4Es. Col Ahmad Atef, the first Egyptian pilot to shoot down an Israeli Phantom II, then became CO of the EAF's first Phantom II unit!

Egypt's shift from a close strategic partnership with the Soviet Union to an alliance with the USA led to some interesting episodes during the training of MiG-21 pilots. Kadri el-Hamid was one of the first, being sent to Williams Air Force Base, Arizona. He recalled;

'We had our course there, and I won the Top Gun award among all the foreign pilots. The colonel had good words for us, and said how he was struck by our standard of flying. The pilots in the (American training) squadron thought we would be

This fine photograph of EAF MiG-21MF serial number 8688 was taken on 6 August 1975. It still wears the standard Soviet two-colour camouflage scheme as applied prior to the jet's delivery to Egypt (*EAF*)

This EAF MiG-21MF was photographed in flight during the joint US-Egyptian Exercise *Bright Star 82*. The jets displays the 'tiger stripe' two-colour pattern camouflage applied in Egypt (*US DoD*)

A post-1973 photograph of MiG-21RF serial number 8506. The RF was a version of the MiG-21R that was built specially for Egypt and flown by No 26 Sqn, based at Inshas, during the October War. Short range and vulnerability to Israeli SAMs prevented the type from playing a more prominent role (*Tom Cooper collection*)

no good because the Israelis said that they had shot down many Egyptians. They in turn would not admit that they had lost aeroplanes in action against us. So after the course the American pilots told us, "You people have a golden hand."

The supply of spares, additional equipment and upgrades for the ageing MiG-21s was almost a bigger

problem than finding replacement aircraft. After the break with the USSR, Egypt's MiGs were initially kept going with spares from unnamed 'friendly Arab countries'. China, and perhaps Yugoslavia, represented other sources of vital spares, but India, despite its long-established relationship with the EAF, was unable to help because of Soviet pressure. So Egypt approached Rolls-Royce, Ferranti and Smiths Industries in the UK, and by 1978, EAF MiG-21s were said to have better British navigation-attack systems than frontline RAF aircraft.

By that time Egypt had fought a brief and largely successful border war with neighbouring Libya. This conflict was a direct result of President Sadat's visit to Israel in 1977, which caused outrage across most of the Arab world. In July 1977, thousands of Libyan protesters initiated a 'March on Cairo', moving towards the Egyptian border. Sadat put the Egyptian Army and Air Force on alert. Libyan leader Col Moamer al Qaddafi ordered an attack on several border posts, and in response an Egyptian armoured brigade moved towards the frontier, while an EAF operational group, under Maj Gen Adel Nasr, prepared for war.

On the morning of 21 July a formation of Su-20s, escorted by MiG-21s, attacked Libyan Army bases and radar stations near the border,

A true survivor – MiG-21F-13, serial number 5403, was on UARAF strength in June 1967, and was still with the EAF in the early 1980s, when it is believed to have formed part of No 102 Air Brigade. It displays the latest three-colour Nile camouflage scheme (*Lon Nordeen*)

Photographed in 1981, this dual-control MiG-21UM (serial number 5654) trainer and pilot testing aircraft was based at Mansourah with No 104 Air Brigade from 1970 onwards. The Winged Horus badge displayed on the jet's nose may be a brigade motif (*Lon Nordeen*)

while Egyptian tanks attacked the town of Musaid. Once this first phase of the operation was concluded, a second wave of EAF fighter-bombers struck Gamal Abdel Nasser air base near Benghazi and another base at al-Kurta, where seven Libyan fighters were claimed destroyed on the ground. Libya tried to hit back, and a formation of Mirage 5s, supported by ECM-equipped Mi-8s, attacked Egyptian positions along the border. The

EAF MiG-21MF serial number 8676 was photographed beside an Egyptian Mirage and F-4 Phantom II at an air force air day in the 1990s. All three aircraft have high visibility orange panels outlined in black (*authors' collections*)

next morning the EAF repeated the attack on Gamal Abdel Nasser base, but this time Libyan Air Force (LARAF) fighters were waiting. Two Mirage 5DEs clashed with escorting MiG-21s, shooting down one in a short dogfight. On 22 and 23 July LARAF aircraft tried to strike targets inside Egypt, but each time the EAF was ready. By the

morning of the 24th three or four Libyan Mirages and one MiG-23 had been shot down by EAF interceptors and air defences. Now, however, Sadat ordered an end to Egyptian military action.

Despite the cease-fire, skirmishes continued. In 1979 two LARAF MiG-23MSs engaged two EAF MiG-21MFs which had been modified to carry American AIM-9P missiles. It proved to be a tactical error for the Libyan pilots to try manoeuvring with the more nimble Egyptian fighters. One MiG-23MS was shot down by Maj Sal Mohammad, a highly experienced MiG-21 pilot who had taken part in the Attrition and October Wars, and had twice been shot been down by Israeli Mirages.

The final, and continuing, phase of the MiG-19 and MiG-21 history in Egyptian service opened with Egypt's purchase of Chinese-built versions of these Soviet-designed aircraft. Egypt received its first batch of 40 Shenyang F-6s (licence-built MiG-19s) and two-seat FT-6s in 1979. In turn, Egypt gave one of its mothballed MiG-23s to China. Although by no means modern or advanced, the F-6s enabled EAF fighter pilots to main-

This Shenyang F-6 (serial number 3860) was photographed at Almaza during Egyptian Air Force Day some years after the 1973 war. It displays black-edged yellow identification panels on its tail-fin, fuselage spine and wingtips, as applied during exercises with American forces. Beneath the cockpit, the Islamic declaration of faith – 'There is no god other than God and Muhammad is the Prophet of God' – appears in small red Arabic writing (*Lon Nordeen*)

American military personnel inspect EAF F-6 serial number 3878 during an Operation *Bright Star* joint exercise in the 1980s (*Lon Nordeen*)

tain their skills, especially as these aircraft were upgraded with US and British weaponry and electronics. Between 1980 and 1990, Egypt also purchased more than 100 Shenyang F-7s – licence-built versions of the Soviet MiG-21F-13.

Although possession of a mixture of combat aircraft caused logistical and maintainance problems, it also gave the EAF what its senior officers described as 'the best *Red Flag* in the world'. This was of particular benefit in terms of training.

EAF MiG-21MFs emerge from an underground hanger at Aswan airport, in Egypt, in 2000. Aswan is also a major military base in the south of the country (*Sherif Sharmy*)

SYRIA KEEPS FIGHTING

'Always be faster, smarter and trickier' was the basic lesson which Syrian MiG-21-pilots learned from their confrontation with the Israelis. During the October War they mastered the art of flying the MiG-21 in air combat, especially at slow speed and low level, making extensive use of the turning capabilities of their aircraft to achieve better air combat results. Without doubt the Arabs closed the gap with the Israelis, but they still lacked a good air-to-air missile. While the Israelis were now armed with the much-improved AIM-9D Sidewinder and Shafrir 2, both of which were vastly superior to any version of the R-13 M, the Arabs never receive any kind of upgraded version of the 'Atoll'.

On the other hand the MiG-21MF did have a cannon, and a relatively large percentage of kills by Arab MiG-21 pilots were achieved with guns during the October 1973 War. Israeli F-4Es, although less manoeuvrable and usually carrying much heavier loads than the MiG-21s, also possessed better avionics. In addition, their communications equipment always provided crews with better awareness. Yet the MiG was not really built for dogfighting. Due to a very rudimentary artificial-feel flight control system, it always suffered from heavy stick forces during turns, and although hard turning was an arena in which this aircraft excelled, pilots found such manoeuvres exhausting.

Nor did the better instantaneous turn rate of the MiG-21MF guarantee any advantage, as the Arabs' opponents usually had similar capabilities, albeit at higher speeds. In combat, an aircraft pursued by a MiG-21 should enter the tightest possible turn and keep turning. The MiG would inevitably fall back, unable to maintain speed because its delta wings acted like a huge air brake. The MiG-21MF was superior at slower speeds, where it could use its manoeuvring flaps because the airframe was otherwise stall-free. But it took time for the Arabs to learn how to employ these capabilities. That they had done so by 1973 was demonstrated by their successes in the October War.

But by 1979 the situation had changed. The MiG-21PFMA and

A Syrian Air Force MiG-21MF sits inside its hardened shelter at Hama air base in 1974. Although the Syrians' hardened hangers were covered in a layer of earth and their openings were painted with a camouflage pattern, they were much simpler structures than those built in Egypt after the Six Day War (*authors' collections*)

Syrian MiG-21F-13 on display at the Military Museum in Damascus before it was repainted. If the camouflage pattern is original, this aircraft could be one of those MiG-21F-13s rushed to Syria from East Germany and Hungary to replace losses in October 1973. The bright green blotches were probably added in Syria, since they also appear on other types of SyAAF aircraft, including helicopters. Some were test-flown by East German pilots in Syria, although it is not known whether they flew combat sorties (*via Tom Cooper*)

The Syrian Air Force CO thanks Hero of the Soviet Union, Konstantin Sukhov (left), for his help in 1989. Sukhov had served as the chief Soviet air combat adviser in Syria from 1973 to 1975, and had himself been a fighter ace during World War 2, with 22 victories to his credit (*authors' collections*)

A pair of Syrian Air Force MiG-21UMs sit outside their hardened hanger at Hama in 1974. Hama was not a major frontline airfield during the October 1973 War, although aircraft based here did help protect Syria's vulnerable coastline (*authors' collection*)

MF remained the Syrians' main fighters, only slowly being replaced by the MiG-23MS, which still had the same weapons system. Meanwhile, the Israelis had introduced the much more advanced F-15A Eagle and were about to get the F-16A Fighting Falcon. Furthermore, Syrian MiG-21s would soon engage the Israelis over Lebanon, where Syrian radar coverage was poor and their intercept-control system not fully developed. They would also face a high-tech air-combat system which included AEW aircraft, communication and radar-jamming aircraft, advanced and reliable all-aspect air-to-air missiles and fighters that could out-fly and out-gun the MiG-21 by a substantial margin.

Syria became involved in Lebanon's terrible civil war in May 1976 when its 3rd Armoured Division was deployed in the south of the country to support the Palestinian Liberation Army against the Christian Phalange Party, which was in turn supported by Israel. The position of Syrian troops in Lebanon soon became precarious and they requested air support. This inevitably led to clashes with the IDF/AF, which already regarded the skies over Lebanon as its own.

By 1979, the SyAAF had almost 200 MiG-21s of various types, only 60 to 70 per cent of which were fully operational. Up to 80 airframes, mostly of the older versions, had replaced losses in 1973, and these were held back in reserve. So the MiG-21PFMA/MF and a few MiG-21SMTs provided the main interceptor component, while examples of the superior MiG-21bis were still scarce. The Soviets were also slow to deliver more potent R-13M and R-13R air-to-air missiles to Syria, and would not deliver any R-60s. Consequently, the technology available to SyAAF MiG-21s was essentially the same as that used during 1973, and its fighters were not capable of operating independently over Lebanon due to their lack of advanced radar and communications systems.

Not surprisingly, losses mounted from the first engagement in July 1979. May 1982 saw no less than 20 MiG-21s shot down in a dozen air battles over Lebanon. These included one MiG-21MF which stalled while trying to tackle a slow-flying Israeli reconnaissance UAV. In exchange, the SyAAF downed just one A-4 Skyhawk. For SyAAF MiG-21 personnel, the brief conflict in June 1982 was no less painful. Although flown by some of the most experienced Syrian pilots, the MiG-21 was simply no match for the air combat system deployed by the IDF/AF.

A heavy blow was suffered on 6 June when Maj Bassam Hamshu was scrambled with a section of MiG-21SMTs from Dumayr air base. Only 14 minutes into the flight, his formation was intercepted by four F-15As and within seconds Hamshu had been shot down and killed. At the time, he was the top Arab ace with seven confirmed aerial kills and one air-to-ground victory to his credit.

On the afternoon of 9 June three squadrons of SyAAF MiG-21s were scrambled to intercept Israeli aircraft attacking Syrian SAM sites in the Bekaa Valley. Although they surprised the enemy, IDF/AF F-15s and F-16s were well placed to ambush them. In the ensuing dogfights at least ten MiG-21s were shot down, three by a single F-15. In exchange, only one F-15D was damaged. Another tragedy stuck when the SyAAF pilots disengaged at very low altitude. The MiG-21bis of Col

Fayez Mansour was shot down by a machine-gun mounted on a Syrian Army tank in the Kanakir area. Mansour was another highly experienced SyAAF pilot with four confirmed kills to his credit.

The situation the next day was not very different, and 14 MiG-21s were lost, with many pilots. But this time the SyAAF ground control managed to get two very-low flying MiG-21MFs into the areas where Israeli F-4 and A-4 fighter-bombers were operating. Two Phantom IIs were attacking an air defence site when, for unknown reasons, one lost power in its left engine. The Israelis broke off their attack and turned for home. This enabled the MiG-21MFs to intercept and down the crippled jet with cannon fire. The Israeli crew ejected and was soon recovered by a helicopter.

Not until 11 June could the SyAAF respond in a more organised manner. That day, the MiG-23MSs and MiG-23MFs were to provide stand-off escort and keep Israeli F-15s away from several MiG-23BNs and Su-22s strike packages escorted by MiG-21s. The first waves of Syrian aircraft reached their targets largely undisturbed, but then the IDF/AF begun stacking sections of F-16s along the Syrian border. Forced to defend the vulnerable fighter-bombers, six MiG-21s were lost in a series of dogfights. In return, only one F-4E was claimed as shot down.

These battles over Lebanon showed the SyAAF that the MiG-21 in its basic form was largely obsolete when pitted against F-15s and F-16s. As a result, MiG-23s shouldered the burden of air warfare against the Israelis. However, the Syrians still occasionally scrambled MiG-21s over Lebanon. For example, when a pair of MiG-23s intercepted and downed an Israeli RF-4E on 9 October 1982, they were supported by two MiG-21MFs which engaged F-15s, buying enough time for the MiG-23s to finish off the Phantom II. The Syrian fighters escaped undamaged, but this was the swan song of the MiG-21 as an interceptor in SyAAF service.

An unidentified SyAAF pilot and his fully armed MiG-21MF, serial number 2349. During the fighting over Lebanon, the Syrians were blinded, jammed, out-manoeuvred and outgunned by the Israelis, who also had far better intelligence about their opponents. Nevertheless, Syrian MiG pilots never stopped flying and fighting, and even gave the Israelis some surprises (Tom Cooper collection)

Although the IDF/AF deny losing any aircraft in air combat over Lebanon in 1982, Syrian MiG-21s scored at least two confirmed kills. They included this F-4E shot down on 10 June 1982, the wreckage of which was eventually found by Syrian troops (Tom Cooper collection)

This line-up of six MiG-21bis were photographed in the USSR shortly before their delivery to Syria in the summer of 1982. Most of the replacements for MiG-21s lost over Lebanon came from Libya, which donated almost its entire fleet of MiG-21MFs and MiG-21bis to the SyAAF in exchange for the loan of instructors and maintenance personnel (via Tom Cooper)

WARS IN THE GULF

By 1980, 90 MiG-21MFs and a few MiG-21F-13s formed the main strength of the Iraqi Air Force/Air Defence Force (IrAF/ADC). At the time, MiG-21s were operated by the 5th, 9th, 12th, 17th and 18th Sqns. A small number of MiG-21Rs were also flown by a flight of the 1st Fighter-Reconnaissance Squadron, which had a few Hunters and was in the process of acquiring MiG-25Ps and MiG-25RBs.

The main Iraqi MiG-21 bases were al-Hurriyah, near Kirkuk, al-Gayar, near Mosul, Raschid and Habbaniyah, in central Iraq, Ubeydah Ibn-Jarrah and Salman Pak, in south-eastern Iraq, and al-Shoibiyah and Jalibah, in southern Iraq. One flight of the 84th Sqn, otherwise equipped with the MiG-23MS, was periodically stationed at one of the airfields of the H-3 complex in western Iraq, which were used as maintenance and training bases during the war with Iran.

For most of the 1970s, the IrAF developed new tactics based on experience from the October War. It was supported in this endeavour by foreign instructors, although, contrary to what is usually reported, Iraqi MiG-21 pilots were more often trained by Indian rather than by Pakistani or Soviet instructors during this period. In fact the Indian Air Force (IAF) had up to 120 instructors in Iraq from the late 1960s onwards, giving basic flying and interceptor training, as well as at the staff college. Some Iraqi pilots and technicians were also sent to India, where no less than 79 training facilities trained foreign pilots.

Work in Iraq was welcomed by Indian pilots, for they could save money, the way of life was not arduous and there were no religious restrictions like those encountered in Saudi Arabia and some other countries. In fact Iraq was considered a moderate Arab state, without religious fanaticism, and cooperation was usually described as good.

For most of the 1970s IrAF units were limited in the number of flying hours available to them, and the type of training allocated. Furthermore, as Ba'ath Party influence spread, flying personnel were given more lessons in political science than flying. Despite the fact that IAF instructors were attached to every major Iraqi air base, their influence remained limited. They did not draft operational doctrines, although the Indians did keep detailed notes concerning Arab experiences in 1967 and 1973, as well as those of the Iraqis during the war with Iran. Generally, the IrAF's operational philosophy was developed by the Iraqis themselves.

The Indians did, however, teach the Iraqis how to aggressively manoeuvre their MiG-21s at low level, thus making them less dependent on ground control. Like the Iraqis, the IAF used point-defence MiG-21 interceptors to defend huge areas, most of which were poorly covered by radar. Furthermore, the Indians had developed low-speed combat manoeuvres for MiG-21s, which they deployed with considerable success against the Pakistani Air Force during their conflict in December 1971. The Indians also taught bomb-tossing and low-level rocket-attack techniques, which enabled the Iraqis to develop their own tactics for MiG-21s.

This blurred but interesting photograph shows an Iraqi Air Force MiG-21MF, serial number 1190, from the second batch supplied to the IrAF in 1974. It still wears the camouflage scheme applied before delivery, and is armed with UB-16 launch pods for unguided 57 mm rockets (*Tom Cooper collection*)

Those pilots confident enough to fly like the Indians used the tactics against the Iranians. Consequently, the Iranian Air Force soon learned to respect the MiG-21 as an opponent.

Just as the best Syrian pilots could not overcome Israel's technological superiority, so the Iraqis continued to experience problems with the MiG-21, despite being spirited fliers using manoeuvrable aircraft.

The technological superiority of Iranian F-4Es and F-14As over Iraqi MiG-21MFs remained immense. Previous American and Israeli experience had been built into the aircraft delivered to Iran, and had also been taught to crews training to fly these types. As was the case with Syrian MiGs, the IrAF MiG-21MFs used in the 1980s were much the same as those flown by North Vietnamese pilots against US fighters in South-east Asia in 1972. The only Iranian equivalent was the F-5E, although it was much better armed than the MiG-21.

Soviet influence increased from 1979, when a large group of instructors arrived in Iraq, along with MiG-25s. They were initially based at al-Shoibiyah in the south. The Soviets also deployed some MiG-21bis, and these apparently participated in aerial combat during the early stages of the war with Iran, although without positive results. In addition to problems with the R-13 missile, IrAF and IAF experience with the 23 mm GSh-23 gun was not good, as an ex-Indian MiG-21 instructor explained;

'The GSh-23 shells did have a higher impact energy than those fired by the US M61. However, given the faster firing rate, the M61 would likely score more hits, and – carrying more ammunition – fighters armed with the 20 mm Vulcan gun had a better combat endurance. The essence was that it was critical to teach MiG-21MF pilots not to fire the cannon unless the target was within a certain crossing angle – the ideal angle was less than 60 degrees.'

Given their average proficiency, Iraqi MiG-21 pilots were advised to avoid engagements with F-14s and even F-4Es whenever possible, unless they enjoyed the advantage of surprise. But the MiG-21MF's poor avionics meant this was not always possible. Too often, the first sign of an F-14-attack came when an Iraqi aircraft was blown apart by a long-range air-to-air missile. Consequently, IrAF MiG-21MFs and MiG-21Rs suffered heavy losses even before the war began. On 10 September 1980,

In 1979, the Soviet Union made delivery of MiG-25s to Iraq conditional upon a regiment of 24 Soviet-flown MiG-21MFs being stationed at al-Shoibiyah air base, near Basra. One of the Soviet-flown aircraft is pictured here. During skirmishes between Iraq and Iran in August 1980, the Iranians noticed the aggressiveness of these pilots, and consequently al-Shoibiyah was one of the Iranian Islamic Republic Air Force's first targets on 22 September 1980 (*Tom Cooper collection*)

two IrAF MiG-21Rs were shot down by F-14s of what was now the Islamic Republic of Iran Air Force (IRIAF) while on a reconnaissance mission inside Iranian airspace. By the 17th four more had been lost to F-4s.

IN COMBAT WITH ALI-CATS

IrAF MiG-21s flew a number of sorties during the initial Iraqi strikes on 22 September and during the following days. On the afternoon of the 24th four MiG-21s and four Su-22s were detected by IRIAF F-14s closing some 12 miles (20 km) west of Vahdati air base, near Dezful. The Tomcats were in a 'combat spread' formation, cruising at 40,000 ft (12,000 m), and the Iraqi formation was at low-level, flying 'welded wing' in echelon. The leader of the Iranian pair led his wingman down to 20,000 ft (6000 m) before opening fire from a range of seven miles (12 km). This was far beyond the MiG-21s' ability to respond. Each Tomcat fired one AIM-7E-4 – one at the lead MiG and one at a Sukhoi.

The Iraqis never detected the attack and took no evasive action before the first Sparrow slammed into the lead MiG-21MF, demolishing it. The Sparrow fired by the Iranian wingman lost its lock and went ballistic. But two of the remaining Iraqi pilots turned into the Tomcats, initiating a high-speed dogfight. As the Tomcats turned left, the MiGs climbed, but as the Iraqi fighters lost speed they entered an arena where the F-14A excelled – low-speed manoeuvring. Within seconds the first MiG was outmanoeuvred and shot down by a Sidewinder. The second MiG got away only because the Iranian wingman suffered an engine stall and his leader abandoned the possibility of a third kill to help the younger pilot.

Barely 24 hours later, IrAF MiG-21s bounced a pair of F-5Es and claimed both shot down. But a far more typical air combat for this period of the war developed on 25 September when at least 12 IrAF MiG-21MFs and MiG-23MS intercepted a large formation of IRIAF Phantom IIs after they had bombed the al-Taqaddum air base west of Baghdad. During a series of chaotic engagements, four MiG-21s and one MiG-23 were shot down in exchange for two F-4s damaged.

On 26 October IrAF MiG-21s struck back. At 0910 hrs, two MiG 21s, probably Russian-flown, took of from Shoibiyah air base to escort two MiG-23BNs in an attack on Abadan, which was already besieged by Iraqi troops. Ten minutes later, while still 21 miles (34 km) from their target, the Iraqi formation was detected by two F-14As on a CAP well inside Iranian airspace. The jets moved forward to intercept, and their leader launched his first AIM-7E-4 from a range of seven miles (12 km), followed by two other Sparrows fired by the wingman several seconds later. The first Iraqi MiG-21 was destroyed by a direct hit, while the other two missiles missed due to guidance data-link problems. The Iraqi pilots never saw their attackers, and the sudden destruction of one aircraft prompted the whole formation to return to base.

On 25 September 1980, a formation of 20 Iranian Phantom IIs bombed al-Hurriyah air base on the outskirts of Kirkuk, in northern Iraq, and this reconnaissance photograph was taken by an Iranian RF-5A after the strike. Note the bomb crater on top of the hardened aircraft shelter, which has been cracked but not penetrated. The two IrAF MiG-21s with under-wing drop tanks parked outside apparently escaped damage. Due to the huge area they had to defend, IrAF MiG-21s were regularly seen carrying three auxiliary fuel tanks and only two air-to-air missiles (*Farzad Bishop collection*)

The situation was rarely different when Iraqi MiG-21s encountered Iranian Phantom IIs flown by highly experienced pilots with extensive training in the USA or in Israel. Nevertheless, the IrAF defended Baghdad enthusiastically. On 29 September 1980 no less than 12 MiG-21MFs and six MiG-23MS scrambled to intercept eight Phantom IIs approaching targets in the area. Despite closing from three directions under constant GCI guidance, the Iraqi formations were detected by the Iranian Phantom IIs' APX-70 'Combat Tree' IFF interrogator system. Two Sparrows fired at one of the MiG-23s proved to be enough to scatter them and spoil the interception. None of the MiGs reached a position from which it could attack.

During the late 1980 rainy season, fighting quietened down, but from January 1981 both sides unleashed offensives and counter-offensives. In April the IRIAF started its next series of counter-air strikes, hitting a number of Iraqi air bases. The first was an ultra-long-range strike by eight IRIAF Phantom IIs on H-3/al-Walid, in western Iraq. Here, Iranian F-4s achieved complete surprise, simultaneously bombing and strafing all three airfields in the complex. Among the Iraqi aircraft destroyed on the ground were four MiG-21MFs.

The Iranian offensive continued with strikes against IrAF bases along the border with Iran. On 25 April, Phantom IIs from Hamadan hit Shoibiyah and shot down one of the defending MiG-21s using guns. In the afternoon, another MiG-21 was shot down by F-4s in combat near Basra, the pilot being captured. Next morning, following a strike on Ubeydah Ibn-Jarrah air base, F-4Es used their 'Combat Tree' and ASX-1 TISEO equipment to down a defending MiG-21MF and a MiG-23MS.

Shocked by these losses the IrAF tried hard to make its MiG-21s more effective. In March and April 1981, with French help, the Iraqis wired a number of MiG-21MFs for the MATRA R.550 Magic Mk 1 missile. At the same time a large group of Iraqi pilots took an intensive course in air-to-air combat based on French manuals. These MiGs, and their pilots, became operational in late March 1981, and in their first encounter with Iranian Phantom IIs proved exceptionally dangerous. Nevertheless, one was shot down by gunfire from an F-4E, while the second hit the same Phantom II with an R.550 and damaged it severely.

The Iranians did not become aware of the new weapon until early May 1981, when Iraqi MiG-21s equipped with R.550s became more aggressive. The IrAF started deploying large groups of MiG-23BNs, escorted by Magic-armed MiG-21s, around Qasr i-Shirin. Within a week the MiG-21s had shot down two F-4Es, two F-5Es and one AH-1J for the loss of one MiG-21. On 6 May, Iranian Phantom IIs forward-deployed at Vahdati shot down another MiG-21, but the IrAF then increased the pressure. Over the following four days two more F-4Es and F-5Es were downed, and the Iraqis virtually achieved local air superiority. Iranian pilots later admitted they had failed because they had believed their own propaganda about Iraqi pilots being cowards that were unwilling to fight.

These heavy losses came as a shock to the IRIAF High Command, and on 15 May ten F-14As were deployed to Vahdati to counter the new threat. The first combat between Tomcats and a formation of Iraqi MiG-21s and MiG-23s that same afternoon showed how the situation had changed. The Iranian aircraft shot down two MiG-21MFs during a joint patrol, and the IrAF went back onto the defensive. Nevertheless, this was a poor exchange for the heavy Iranian losses of previous weeks.

THE LOST IRAQI ACES

Several Iraqi MiG-21 pilots rose to prominence during the war with Iran. The best known was Lt (later Col) Mohammed 'Sky Falcon' Rayyan, who flew MiG-21MFs in 1980-81, and claimed two confirmed kills against Iranian F-5Es in 1980. With the rank of captain, Rayyan qualified on MiG-25Ps in late 1981 and went on to claim another eight kills, two of which are confirmed, before being shot down and killed by IRIAF F-14s and F-5s in 1986. Capt Omar Goben claimed two F-5Es and one F-4E in 1980 before transferring to MiG-23MS and then MiG-23MF/MLs. He survived the war but was killed in January 1991 flying a MiG-29 in combat with USAF F-15Cs. Col K Wallid, another former MiG-21 pilot who commanded the IrAF MiG-29 wing in 1991, was also shot down by US F-15Cs prior to defecting to Saudi Arabia.

Like many others, Capt Fuad Tait flew MiG-21s early in his career, before being captured by the Iranians after his Mirage F1EQ-5 was shot down by F-14s over the Persian Gulf. On 3 October 1980, he was leading a pair of MiG-21MFs on a hit and run bombing mission over the southern front when two F-4Ds pounced on them. Tait explained what happened next;

'Our aircraft were armed with two small Russian-made FAB 250-kg bombs each and a full load of gun ammunition. We were underway at a very low level when two F-4Ds appeared seemingly out of nowhere to attack us. I ordered my wingman to jettison the bombs and follow me, but it was too late to defend ourselves as the Phantom IIs were already on our tails and firing missiles. We were both shot down within seconds and barely managed to eject.'

Because of persistent problems with the R-13 and R-13R missiles, and amazed by the performance of the AIM-9P in Iranian service, the Iraqis tried to obtain some Sidewinders. Tait explained, 'In 1983, we purchased 200 AIM-9B rounds from Jordan, produced no less than 15 years earlier, in exchange for oil and two Iranian F-5Es'. One of these had been flown to Iraq by IRIAF defector Lt S Doakhan, who had delivered the jet complete with two AIM-9Ps. The Iraqis sent the two Sidewinders to the USSR, starting a rumour that the Iranians had also delivered an intact F-14A with AIM-54A Phoenix missiles to the Soviets. Another F-5E was captured intact after a forced landing near Basra. Tait continues;

'We took these Sidewinders into service in the hope that they would place our MiG-21 pilots on a more even footing with Iranian F-4s and F-5s in air-to-air combat. In the following 12 months our MiG-21s, armed with US-made Sidewinders, shot down five IRIAF aeroplanes, including two F-5s, one F-4D, one C-130H and a Bell 214C helicopter. We finally replaced them with a new batch of 70 R.550 Magic Mk 1s, supplied by the French in 1984.'

Capt Daryush 'Z', a highly experienced ex-IRIAF F-4 pilot who encountered the MiG-21 in combat, gave an Iranian perspective on air combat with the IrAF;

'We had been trained by the Americans, and some of us flew both the MiG-21s and MiG-23s on secret evaluation flights in the USA in the

1970s, so we knew a lot about the MiG-21s. The IrAF MiG-21s were very good point-defence fighters but poor fighter-bombers. The MiG-21 could turn. To this day I'm convinced it was their best dogfighter. That is, at least, after they replaced R-13s with Magic air-to-air missiles.'

That the MiG-21MF had serious design flaws was confirmed by Lt Tariq al-Dinmaruf, a former IrAF MiG-21-pilot who shot down an IRIAF F-5E on 30 September 1980 using 23 mm guns before being captured by the Iranians in April 1981. He said;

'The MiG-21 was a pleasure to fly and an outstanding fighter. It was light and nimble, but poorly armed. The ASP-PFD gunsight was rugged, simple, and it worked. The R-13A missile, on the other hand, was unreliable, and could not deliver the kill. The Egyptians even tried to sell us their remaining R-13s to get rid of them, but we turned the offer down. The 23 mm GSh-23 cannon was a devastating weapon, utterly reliable and ready, even if the usual burst would not cause sufficient damage to an F-4 or F-14 to shoot them down.'

THE MiG-21 IN LATER YEARS

In June 1982, an IrAF captain defected with his MiG-21 to Syria. During his interrogation, the officer revealed that since the start of the war the IrAF had lost no less than 98 fighters (including MiG-25s) in air-to-air combats with Iranian F-4s and F-14s. He also reported that 33 Iraqi pilots had been killed in air combat and that, by the time of his escape, only three IrAF squadrons were able to fly offensive operations. The pilot also reported that by February 1982 Iraq had ordered no less than 300 new fighters and 100 new helicopters, mainly from the USSR but also from China.

Most observers still believe that no new weapons or spare parts were delivered to Iraq by the USSR until 1983. However, the vast majority of Soviet instructors still in-country continued doing what they could to help. In the weeks immediately before the war, the Soviets had established an air bridge to deliver huge amounts of spares and weapons to the IrAF. Although arms deliveries became irregular throughout most of 1980 and 1981, they were never discontinued.

Nevertheless, anti-Soviet sentiment increased even in the IrAF, as former Iraqi MiG-21 pilot Capt Amir explained;

'By the mid-1980s, the Russians were everywhere in Iraq, regardless of the fact that we were never fully able to trust them. They liked to give orders to the Arabs. For us, taking orders from Russians was distasteful, and we felt the sooner they left Iraq the better it would be.'

Persistent quarrels and Moscow's refusal to supply more advanced aircraft, or even readily available 'downgraded' ones, in the numbers requested, finally forced Baghdad to turn elsewhere. In 1982, Egypt started buying F-7B fighters from

Iranian authorities carefully examined all the Iraqi aircraft that were shot down behind Iranian lines. This Iraqi MiG-21 was downed by Iranian SAMs in the Faw area in February 1986 (*Farzad Bishop collection*)

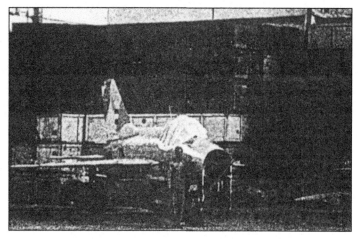

From early 1983 onwards, about 40 Shenyang F-7Bs were delivered by China to Iraq via Egypt and Saudi Arabia. One of the first is seen here in this grainy photograph taken in 1984 at al-Raschid air base, south of Baghdad (*Tom Cooper collection*)

The so-called Second Gulf War in 1991 was much shorter than the Iran-Iraq War, but Iraqi MiG-21s fared no better. Two were shot down in air combat with US Navy F/A-18A Hornets, 16 were destroyed on the ground and several were captured at airfields in southern Iraq. Most were seized at Tallil and Jalibah air-bases, this MiG-21UM, serial number 21073, being one of those captured by troops of the US Army's 24th Mechanized Division. The IrAF operated at least two-dozen of these aircraft. A shell through the fuselage spine put an end to the flying career of this example, which was subsequently destroyed by the Americans before they pulled back to Kuwait (*US DoD*)

China and, as Egyptian pilots were already flying with the IrAF, the Iraqis learned about this Saudi-financed deal. Within months a similar arrangement was concluded, again with Saudi financing, for the delivery of 40 F-7Bs to Iraq.

The J-6s and F-7Bs delivered to Iraq were very basic, equipped only with PL-2 missiles (R-13 copies). Nevertheless, the air force needed quantity rather than quality, and so these aircraft were accepted into service. But the 40 J-6s did not last long, and as early as 1984 were being mainly used for advanced training. The F-7Bs, however, entered service with the 5th and 6th Sqns, and remained operational until 2003. Flying F-7Bs from Egypt to Iraq over Saudi Arabia proved complicated, difficult and dangerous. The Iraqis, therefore, deployed three An-12BPs to Jordan, where the transports were painted in Royal Jordanian Air Force markings. They ferried F-7Bs from China to Jafr airfield, in southern Jordan, where they were assembled and tested for the IrAF.

In response to the deal with China, the Soviets finally supplied a batch of 25 MiG-21bis to Iraq in February 1983. Still armed with R-13 missiles, they barely replaced Iraq's losses. Subsequently, another batch followed, along with some R-60 missiles, but by the time they entered service they were already considered second-line assets.

Before the Chinese J-6s and F-7s arrived in Iraq, the MiG-21MFs continued to encounter problems. In October 1982, the Iranians initiated Operation *Muslim Ibn-Aqil* in the Qasr i-Shirin area. The IrAF, still licking its wounds after terrible losses and hampered by weather and terrain, was slow to respond, and its MiG-21s were rarely seen. However, later in October Lt Ahmed Salem downed an Iranian Army AH-1J Cobra, although he almost stalled while manoeuvring to keep it in sight.

The following month, during battles provoked by an Iranian offensive on the northern front, IrAF MiG-21 units again suffered considerable losses, especially the 12th and 17th Sqns. On the 16th, a MiG was shot down by Iranian Phantom IIs using Sidewinders, while another was lost to an MIM-23 Hawk SAM. On the 20th a MiG-21 fell to AIM-9s fired by an F-5E, and the following day one of four MiG-21MFs escorting a formation of helicopters taking two Iraqi generals on an inspection of the front was shot down by an AIM-54A fired by an F-14A.

There were no successes to balance these losses, despite IrAF claims that three Iranian F-14s, eight F-4s, five F-5Es and at least 20 helicopters had been downed.

Iranians continued encountering Iraqi MiG-21s until the end of the war, but much less often. Yet, by 1991, the MiG-21 was still the most numerous interceptor and fighter-bomber in Iraqi service, with some 120 F-13s, MFs, PFs, PFMs, PFMAs, UTIs and UMs remaining. In addition, two squadrons were flying F-7Bs. The exact disposition and strength of these units is not known, but none had a full complement of 12 jets. By January 1991 all operated in flights well-dispersed across 30 or so airfields.

This battered MiG-21PFMA or possibly a MiG-21R (serial number 21302) was one of the few examples photographed by US troops in 1991 prior to it being destroyed (*US DoD*)

Iraqi MiG-21s did not see much fighting during the Second Gulf War, which saw the liberation of Kuwait. Their best-known engagement involved a short clash with US Navy F/A-18A Hornets on the morning of 17 January 1991. Their participation is usually ridiculed by western media, but the Iraqi pilots were trying to do what they could in the face of Allied superiority. Nor did they lack ideas.

As a strike package from USS *Saratoga* approached the H-3 complex, four MiG-21s were launched to act as decoys. The bait was accepted and, turning east towards H-2 air base, near al-Rutbah, the MiGs drew the MiG-CAP of four F-14Bs away from the rest of the Navy formation. The Tomcat crews requested permission to fire their AIM-54s, but the mission commander aboard an E-2C refused because his radar could not positively identify the enemy aircraft. Once the F-14Bs were over 60 miles (100 km) from H-3, two further MiG-21s were launched to attack the main strike package, but their pilots flew right into a section of F/A-18 Hornets from VFA-81 and were shot down.

So ended the active participation of Iraqi MiG-21s in the Second Gulf War. Many were subsequently destroyed on the ground, and several were captured by the US Army on Tallil and Jalibah air bases. At Tallil, US forces also found a solitary MiG-21F-13 (F-7B)gate-guard, as well as several MiG-21MFs and a single MiG-21R. All were destroyed before the Americans pulled back into Saudi Arabia. By 1999 there were still between 34 and 36 F-7Bs serving with the IrAF, of which 32 were operational. The MiG-21 was virtually extinct, however.

After the first two Gulf Wars in 1980-1988 and 1991, and numerous US and British air-strikes during the 1990s, only 32 to 34 IrAF F-7Bs remained intact by the time of the Third Gulf War in 2003. Most of these were captured by US troops, including this example at an unnamed airfield in southern Iraq. Interestingly, F-7Bs acted as gate-guards at some larger Iraqi bases, including Tallil (*US DoD*)

APPENDICES

ARAB MIG UNITS AND THEIR DISPOSITIONS

EGYPT

Unit	Type	Base	Other Information
20/21	MiG-19S	Fayid	Ex-Nos 27/29 Sqn in 1965, CO Alaa Barakat; part of 15th Air Brigade (converted to Su-7 after June 1967 war, remaining aircraft and MiG-19s from Syria and Iraq held back for internal defence)
	MiG-19S	Hurghada	Separate flight based at Hurghada before Six Day war, CO Said Shalash
21	MiG-21PFM	Salihiyah	1969, reconnaissance squadron
	MiG-21RF	Salihiyah	Fighter-reconnaissance squadron; winter 1969-70 and 1978
22	MiG-21	perhaps at Abu Suweir or Jabal Libni	June 1967; perhaps part of 5th Air Brig
25	MiG-21	perhaps at Abu Suweir or Jabal Libni	Before and during Six Day War; perhaps part of 5th Air Brigade (apparently equipped with MiG-17 after Six Day War and based at Quwaysina under CO Alaa Barakat; re-equipped with MiG-21 before or by 1969)
	MiG-21	Inshas	1969-1973 (at least), CO Alaa Shakir; part of 102nd Air Brigade under Nabil Shoukry; half-squadron sent to Hughada ten days before October 1973 War began
26	MiG-21	perhaps at Abu Suweir or Jabal Libni	June 1967; perhaps part of 5th Air Brigade
	MiG-21F-13	Sayah el-Sharif	1969
	MiG-21	Inshas	October 1973, CO Ahmad Anwar; part of 102nd Air Brigade under Nabil Shoukry
27	MiG-19	Fayid	Established 1961, CO Ahmad Dirayni (presumably became 'nameplate' when unit was subsequently divided into two squadrons, Nos 20 and 21, as 15th Air Brigade)
	MiG-21	(unknown)	Re-established after Six Day War
	MiG-21	Abu Hammad	October 1973, CO Kamal Isawy; part of 102nd Air Brigade under Nabil Shoukry
27/29	MiG-19	Fayid	1964, combined squadron because of maintenance problems; CO Alaa Barakat; apparently renumbered as Nos 20/21 Sqn before June 1967
35	MiG-21RF	Sayah el-Sharif	1970-71; Soviet Autonomous Section
40	MiG-21	Inshas and Fayid	June 1967, CO Amosis Azer; perhaps divided between 2nd and 9th Air Brigades
41	MiG-21	perhaps at Abu Suweir or Jabal Libni	June 1967; perhaps part of 5th Air Brigade
42	MiG-21	perhaps at Abu Suweir or Jabal Libni	June 1967; perhaps part of 5th Air Brigade
45	MiG-21	Milayz, Abu Suweir and Inshas	June 1967, CO Abdel Kafi Subhi; those at Milayz and Abu Suweir forming part of 5th Air Brigade, with HQ at Abu Suweir; those at Inshas part of 9th Air Brigade
46	MiG-21	perhaps at Abu Sueir or Jabal Libni	June 1967; perhaps part of 5th Air Brigade
	MiG-21	Mansourah	1970, nightfighter squadron
47	MiG-21	Cairo West	June 1967, CO perhaps Abd al-Hamid Helmy
49	MiG-21		June 1967
137	MiG-19	Kafr Daud	Early 1969; this number perhaps technically an air brigade, not divided into squadrons
'Big'	MiG-21	Cairo West	Surviving MiG-21s from Canal Zone and some other bases assembled into an un-numbered wing or 'big' or 'all-weather' squadron after first series of Israeli strikes during the Six Day War; equivalent of two squadrons; CO Fuad Kamal for first two months; started operations 8 June 1967; one of squadrons probably became No 47
OTU	MiG-21	Kibrit	Up to June 1967, CO el-Masri
	MiG-21 (including UM)	Mansourah and Rahmaniyah	1973 to 1984 at least

UNIDENTIFIED SQUADRON, PROBABLY INCLUDED IN THE ABOVE

?	MiG-21	Hurghada	1969-70; independent squadron not attached to an air brigade; after War of Attrition half squadron relocated to Luxor civilian airport

Unit	Types	Base	Other Information
(AIR BRIGADES/WINGS)			
2	(included some MiG-19a)	Fayid(?)	June 1967
5	MiG-21F-13 and FL	Abu Suweir	June 1967, CO Fuad Kamal; HQ at Abu Suweir; CO Fuad Kamal; comprised two squadrons at Abu Suweir and one at Jabal Libni
7	MiG-21	Cairo West	June 1967
9	MiG-21	Inshas	June 1967, CO Sami Fuad; HQ, Nos 40 and 45 Sqns at Inshas, one at Abu Suweir; became 102nd Air Regiment in 1969
15	MiG-19	Fayid	1965; HQ at Fayid; CO Ahmad Hassan Diwayni; Nos 20/21 combined Squadrons under Alaa Barakat; converted to Su-7 later in 1967, disbanded with introduction of new air brigade numbering system mid-1969
101	MiG-21	Beni Sueif	(or 111?); mid-1969 to 1973 at least; CO Adel Nasr; had probably been the air brigade based at Abu Suweir in June 1967; replaced by Southern Air District 1974
102	MiG-21 (FL, PF and PFM)	Inshas	Spring 1969 onwards; CO Nabil Shoukry; comprising Nos 25, 26 and 27 Sqns; replaced by 149th Air Division October 1974
104	MiG-21 (F-13, PFS, later MF)	Mansourah	Spring 1969 onwards, CO Ahmed Abdul Rahman Nasr; replaced by 139th Air Division October 1974
135	MiG-21MF	Beni Sueif	1970-71; operated by Soviet personnel under Soviet command and control
139	MiG-21	Mansourah	From October 1974
224	MiG-21 and Mirage 5R	(unknown)	Changed from fighter-bomber role 1977 with Su-7 to reconnaissance
South	MiG-21	Luxor	HQ at Luxor; replacing previous 101st or 111th Air Brigade South

SYRIA

Unit	Types	Base	Other Information
5	MiG-21PF		Operational before Six Day War; re-equipped with MiG-21PF after the war
	MiG-21MF (x12)	Damascus International	Operational before 1973 war at Damascus International Airport late summer 1973
7	MiG-21F-13 (x4) and PF (x6)	Latakia	Late summer 1973, probably operated by one flight; also operating large number of MiG-17s in ground attack role
8	MiG-21F-13		Started receiving aircraft 1961
			Re-equipped with MiG-2F-13 after Six Day War
	MiG-21MF (x12)	Marj Ruhayyil	Late summer 1973
9	MiG-21PF		Re-equipped with MiG-21PF after Six Day War
	MiG-21PF (x7)	al-Qusayr	Late summer 1973
	MiG-21PFV		Probably operational before 1973 war
10	MiG-21F-13		Started receiving aircraft 1961
			Re-equipped with MiG-2F-13 after Six Day War
	MiG-21F-13 (x7)	Damascus International	At Damascus International Airport late summer 1973
	MiG-21U (x8)	Jirah	Late summer 1973
11	MiG-21F-13		Started receiving aircraft 1961;re-equipped with MiG-2F-13 after Six Day War
	MiG-21MF (x12)	Khalkhalah	Late summer 1973
	MiG-21MF (x2)	Marj Ruhayyil	Remaining aircraft sent to Marj Ruhayyil and placed under command of the 8th Sqn 12 October 1973
12	MiG-21PF (x11)	Suwaydah	Late summer 1973
	MiG-21PF (x4)	Marj Ruhaytil	Remaining aircraft sent to Marj Ruhayyil and placed under command of 8th Sqn 11 October 1973
54	MiG-21PF		Operational before 1973 war
	MiG-21PF (x10) and F-13 (x3)	al-Qusayr	Late summer 1973, to defend Mediterranean coast
	MiG-21PFV	Abu al-Dahur	Some deployed to Abu al-Dahur September 1973
67	MiG-21F-13		MiG-17 replaced with MiG-21F-13 after Six Day War
	MiG-21F-13 (x11) and U (x1)	Dumayr	Late summer 1973
68	MiG-21F-13		MiG-17 replaced with MiG-21F-13 after Six Day War
	MiG-21F-13 (x5) and PF (x8)	Marj Sultan	Late summer 1973
77	MiG-19S		Operational before Six Day War
	MiG-21PF		Re-equipped with MiG-21PF after Six Day War; remaining MiG-19S transferred to Egypt
	MiG-21F-13 (x10)	al-Qusayr	Late summer 1973

IRAQ

Unit	Types	Base	Other Information
1	MiG-21R		Flown by one flight in 1980; rest of squadron operating Hunter modified to FR 10 standard, and was in the process of acquiring MiG-25P and MiG-25RB
5	MiG-21 (unspecified type)		1980
	F-7B		1991
6	F-7B		1991
9	MiG-21PF (x18)	al-Mezze (Syria)	Arrived 7 October 1973; moved to Dumayr air base within a few days MiG-21 (unspecified type) 1980
11	MiG-19		First Iraqi unit to receive MiG-19 in 1961; aircraft subsequently transferred to Egypt
	MiG-21F-13		Re-equipped with MiG-21 shortly before, during or immediately after the Six Day War
12	MiG-21 (unspecified type)		1980-91 at least
17	MiG-21F-13		First Iraqi unit to receive MiG-21 (x12) in 1962
	MiG-21MF		First Iraqi unit equipped with MiG-21MF; arrived at al-Mezze in Syria 13 October 1973; later moved to Dumayr air base within a few days
	MiG-21MF	al-Hurriyah	In 1980-81
	MiG-21 (unspecified type)		1980-91 at least
18	MiG-21 (unspecified type)		1980-91 at least
24	MiG-21 (unspecified type)		1991
25	MiG-21 (unspecified type)		1991
27	MiG-21 (unspecified type)		1991
28	MiG-21 (unspecified type)		1991
29	MiG-21 (unspecified type)		1991
33	MiG-21 (unspecified type)		1991
34	MiG-21 (unspecified type)		1991
84	MiG-21 (unspecified type)	H-3 (periodically)	Flown by one flight in 1980-91; squadron otherwise equipped with MiG-23MS
?	MiG-21PF		A second unknown squadron became operational with MiG-21PF by spring 1967
?	MiG-19S (x12)		Unknown squadron; operational by 1962

COLOUR PLATES

1

MiG-19S (2921), No 29 Sqn, UARAF, Fayid, Egypt, summer 1965
This is one of several aircraft transferred from the Iraqi Air Force, each of which had the name of an Iraqi city painted in white beneath the cockpit, in this case al-Mawsil (Mosul). At a time when all Egyptian combat aircraft had a bare-metal finish, these MiG-19s arrived in two-tone grey camouflage.

2

MiG-19S (3220), No 20/21 Combined Sqn, UARAF, Hurghada, Egypt, June 1967
Some time after entering Egyptian service, rear fuselage and wingtip identification stripes worn by all Egyptian fighters and ground-attack aircraft since the second half of 1948 were applied to UARAF MiG-19s. These stripes were typically black, although both green and red seem to have been used on occasion. The MiG-19s also boasted a broad green-edged white band. The overall grey colouring of Egypt's MiG-19s would cause identification problem during the Six Day War in June 1967.

3

MiG-19S (2965), No 137 Sqn (possibly nominal air brigade), UARAF, Kafr Daud, Egypt, 1969
A few Egyptian MiG-19Ss survived the Six Day War and were given a camouflage paint scheme within days of the conflict's end. The ex-Iraqi aircraft already had a two-tone grey colour scheme, and there is also debate about whether or not their undersides were actually painted blue, as is suggested in recent evidence from Russia. This aircraft has APU-13 launch rails and is armed with R-3S missiles.

4

F-6 (3802), EAF squadron unknown, Giancalis, Egypt, 1994
Acquired in 1979, Egypt's first batch of 40 Shenyang F-6 licence-built MiG-19s served in at least two frontline combat squadrons. More recently, they have been used for operational training. Note the form of camouflage paint application around the gun muzzle, and also that the lighter grey on the uppersurfaces continues around the undersides. The aircraft's serial was often repeated on the upper side of any drop tank that was carried, the store generally being left in overall bare-metal.

5

FT-6 (3954), EAF operational training unit, base unknown, 1980s
Unlike the two-tone grey camouflage applied to Egyptian F-6s, two-seat FT-6s were supplied in overall very light grey. They are believed to have retained this scheme for some time

6

MiG-21F-13 (5403), UARAF storage, June 1967
This aircraft was from one of the last batches of MiG-21F-13s to be delivered to Egypt before the Six Day War, and may have been stored during that conflict. It certainly survived the campaign (see profile 7), and is seen in typical UARAF markings prior to the Israeli assault of 1967. The aircraft features a high performance bare-metal finish, plus green rear fuselage and wing-tip stripes. The aircraft carries a 490-litre auxiliary fuel-tank beneath the fuselage and has APU-13 launch rails for R-3S (R-13) 'Atoll' missiles.

7

MiG-21F-13 (5403), No 102 Air Brigade (squadron unknown), EAF, Inshas, Egypt, 1981
Having survived the Six Day War, the subsequent War of Attrition and the 1973 October War, this MiG-21F-13 was something of a 'hero aircraft' for the EAF. During the War of Attrition, it almost certainly wore a two-tone camouflage on its uppersurfaces, but shortly before the 1973 conflict it was given the new 'Nile Valley' scheme of sand, slate grey and spinach, with sky blue undersides, along with the new style of national insignia.

8

MiG-21F-13 (66), ex-19th or 29th Sqn, QJA (Algerian Air Force), Inshas, Egypt, July 1967
This Algerian MiG-21F-13 is believed to have formed part of the unnumbered 'big squadron' sent to Egypt towards the end of the Six Day War. It was then given Egyptian markings, serial number and a newly-adopted camouflage scheme, and formed part of the recreated UARAF 'big wings' at Inshas. The aircraft is armed with UB-16 rocket pods, and has a 490-litre centreline drop-tank.

9

MiG-21F-13 (5843), No 26 Sqn, UARAF, Sayah el-Sharif, Egypt, 1969
As part of the élite 'Black Ravens' Squadron, this aircraft has the unit's badge painted on its nose, although it is not certain that all the unit's MiG-21s displayed the marking during this period. The aircraft also has the sand and spinach, with light blue undersides, version of the camouflage applied to Egyptian fighters based at Nile Delta airfields after the Six Day War. It is armed with R-3S missiles on APU-13 launch rails.

10

Shenyang F-7B (4547), 149th Air Division, EAF, Inshas, Egypt, late 1980s
The main visible difference between a MiG-21F-13 and a Chinese licence-built Shenyang F-7B was the latter's sideways opening cockpit canopy. The lighter tone of uppersurface grey continues across the undersides of this aircraft. The black-edged

orange high visibility panels on the fin, fuselage spine and wingtips have been a feature of many Egyptian combat aircraft since Egypt became a US ally. Note that the black edging of the fuselage panel is narrower than the others. The Egyptians - with the help of Saudi finance – were instrumental in the delivery of F-7Bs to Iraq in the 1980s.

11

MiG-21PF (5257), probably No 46 Sqn, UARAF Mansourah, Egypt, 1969

Because the UARAF's frontline aircraft were hurriedly camouflaged with available car paint immediately after the Six Day War, the patterns of such camouflage schemes varied considerably. This version had very broad 'spinach' stripes, whilst the uppersurface colours came a long way down the sides of the fuselage. The aircraft has APU-13 launch rails and an R-3S missile on the underwing pylons.

12

MiG-21PF (6089), EAF unit and location unknown, 1972

Although the EAF had re-adopted its earlier name during 1971, many aircraft continued to have the earlier form of UARAF national markings incorporating two small green stars. This aircraft also has another version of the camouflage hastily applied in the weeks after the end of the Six Day War.

13

MiG-21PF (8105), EAF unit and location unknown, October 1973

A slight variation on the broad-stripe style of camouflage had the uppersurface colours coming no lower down the fuselage than the line of the wings. Immediately after the 1967 war, such colours were added at air brigade or perhaps even squadron level, which resulted in a notable lack of uniformity. Note also the new-style national markings added after 1971. This aircraft is armed with R-3S heat-seeking missiles on APU-13 launch rails and has a bare-metal 450-litre drop tank attached to its centreline pylon. Many Egyptian MiG-21PFs also had cannon pods mounted beneath the front fuselage.

14

MiG-21FL (5207), No 47 Sqn, UARAF, Cairo West, Egypt, June 1967

This aircraft was slightly damaged on the runway at Cairo West on the morning of 5 June 1967, but was repaired and took part in both the War of Attrition and the October 1973 War, surviving both. It is shown here in the overall bare-metal finish common for all Egyptian MiG-21s up to the Six Day War. The two narrow green identification bands around the rear fuselage appear to enclose a broader white band, although this may have been an effect of light in a low-level Israeli reconnaissance photograph. Armed only with a pair of rather ineffective heat-seeking R-3S

missiles (not shown here), the MiG-21FL proved almost powerless as a dogfighter until equipped with a gun-pack beneath the fuselage.

15

MiG-21FL (5860), probably No 45 Sqn, No 9 Air Brigade, UARAF, Inshas, Egypt, 1966

Once again, it is not certain that the rear fuselage identification stripes seen on this jet really enclosed a broader white band. The serial number is also written in very small Arabic numerals, as was seen on some of the first MiG-21s supplied to Egypt. The small black anti-dazzle panel in front of the cockpit on this machine was not common amongst Egyptian MiG-21s during this period, and it may have been a local or personal addition. Once again, this aircraft features APU-13 launch rails carrying R-3S missiles, as well as a 490-litre centreline drop-tank.

16

MiG-21PFM (5072), EAF unit and location unknown, 1973

Although essentially the same as the MiG-21FLs delivered to Egypt before the Six Day War, those airframes arriving after the conflict were generally designated MiG-21PFMs. This aircraft has UB-16 rocket pods mounted beneath the underwing pylons. Note also the massive 'bolt on' GP-9 gun-pod which gave the MiG-21PFM greater punch as a dogfighter, but which also reduced its performance – it is not entirely clear which aircraft carried this pod. The jet's uppersurface camouflage is the new three-tone 'Nile Valley' scheme developed by the Egyptians after they found that the two-colour, factory-applied camouflage worn by the aircraft when they arrived from the USSR was unsuitable in combat.

17

MiG-21PFM (5081), probably No 21 Sqn, UARAF, Salihiyah, Egypt, 1969

This aircraft has what appears to be an early or experimental version of the 'Nile Valley' camouflage scheme, comprising sand, olive green and a light grey-green, with light sky blue undersides. It was possibly developed for the UARAF's elite photo-reconnaissance flight. The jet carries one of the small number of British-built Vicon photo-reconnaissance pods sold to Egypt in 1968. Based upon the dimension and aerodynamics of the standard 490-litre auxiliary tank, it was similarly attached to the centreline fuselage pylon.

18

MiG-21MF (8304), No 135 Air Brigade, UARAF Beni Sueif, Egypt, April-May 1970

The 135th Air Brigade was a Soviet unit under Soviet command, operated by Soviet personnel, although with assistance from UARAF groundcrews. Its aircraft carried Egyptian national markings and UARAF serial numbers, but the aircraft's legal ownership remains unclear.

According to some sources, the aircraft returned to the USSR when the Soviets were sent home by President Sadat, while other sources maintain they remained in Egypt as part of the renamed EAF. It is equally possible that many were not returned from refurbishment when Moscow and Cairo fell out in 1974. Camouflage schemes remained those applied at the Gorky factory in Russia, and they were armed with four R-3R missiles on two APU R-3R launch rails beneath each wing. Note that the centreline 490-litre drop-tank is bare-metal.

19
MiG-21 MF (8410), probably No 104 Air Brigade, UARAF, Mansourah, Egypt, spring 1970
The first batch of MiG-21MFs delivered to Egypt in late 1969 do not seem to have had the camouflage schemes normally applied at the MiG factory. The narrow, or 'tiger-stripe', version of sand and spinach seen on this aircraft was probably applied in Egypt. The jet is armed with R-3S missiles, mounted on APU-3R launch rails.

20
MiG-21MF (8460), EAF unit and base unknown, late 1970s
After the October 1973 War, some Egyptian Air Force units started displaying squadron badges again. These had been extremely rare since the pre-1967 period, and even then they were applied to MiG-17s rather than MiG-21s. Unfortunately, the identification of such badges, including the 'red demon's head' on this aircraft, has not been confirmed. The three-colour 'Nile Valley' camouflage on this aircraft also seems to have been applied to all EAF MiG-21s from the late 1970s onwards. The jet is armed with R-3R missiles on an APU-13MT launch rail under the outer underwing pylons, and R-3Ss on APU-13 launch rails under the inboard pylons. The centreline auxiliary fuel tank is painted the same light blue as the undersides of the MiG. During wartime, such stores remained unpainted due to their short life span.

21
MiG-21R (8501), No 21 Sqn, EAF, Salihiyah, Egypt, early 1973
The newly developed 'Nile Valley' camouflage scheme is particularly clear on this recently delivered reconnaissance aircraft. The fact that the 490-litre drop tanks beneath the wings are azure blue suggests that the jet was not expected to enter combat. Beneath the MiG-21R's fuselage is a Soviet-made Type D daylight photo-reconnaissance pod, which also included flare and chaff dispensers. Finally, note the wingtip aerial containers.

22
MiG-21U (5654), No 104 Air Brigade, EAF, Mansourah, Egypt, 1970
One or two dual-control conversion trainers were attached to each Egyptian fighter air brigade. Their

'Nile Valley' camouflage schemes were the same as those on many operational MiG-21s. The 'Winged Horus' badge on the side of the nose may be a brigade rather than a squadron motif, although this has not been confirmed.

23
MiG-19S (1128), 77th Sqn, SyAAF, probably Dumayr, Syria, early 1967
A small but noticeable distinguishing feature of Syrian Air Force aircraft was the repetition of serial numbers in smaller numerals above the national insignia on their tail fins, which had been done since 1948. Some frontline combat aircraft were also camouflaged, including a number of MiG-19s. This two-colour style had previously been applied to British-built Meteors operated by Syria in the 1950s. Note that the national markings have also been changed from the old type with a green outer ring and red stars to the new style with a red outer ring and green stars in the white ring. This was the Syrian version of the UARAF markings adopted in 1963, which only had two stars.

24
MiG-21F-13 (2540), SyAAF unit unknown, probably al-Mezze, Syria, 1962
The SyAAF's 8th, 10th or 11th Sqns began receiving MiG-21F-13s in 1961, and one unit seems to have been operational in 1962, although its identity remains unknown. At this stage the aircraft still carried the original SyAAF roundels with green outer rings, used from 1948 to 1958 and revived between 1961 and 1963. Unlike Syrian MiG-19s, these MiG-21s retained their high-performance bare-metal finish. This aircraft is armed with R-3S missiles on APU-13 launch rails beneath the underwing pylons.

25
MiG-21F-13 (2190), 67th Sqn, SyAAF, probably Dumayr, Syria, late 1973/early 1974
The camouflage scheme on this aircraft differs from that seen on most other SyAAF MiG-21s during this period because it was one of a handful of machines sent to Syria from the Bulgarian and Hungarian air forces during the October 1973 War, and in its immediate aftermath. The jet is believed to have been flown by both Syrians and Pakistani air force pilots attached to this squadron. It is armed with R-3S missiles on APU-13 launch rails, and has a bare-metal centreline drop-tank.

26
MiG-21PFM (SPS) (1072), SyAAF unit and location unknown, 1968-70
This aircraft's version of the 'sand and spinach' uppersurface camouflage scheme was added in Syria and, as in Egypt, was applied in several local variations. However, the SyAAF only used sand and spinach (the spinach sometimes appearing to have faded to a greenish brown), not the yellow and brown 'sand and stone' also used by Egypt, since air combat in Syria was largely fought over

the country's fertile western areas. The aircraft is armed with R-3S missiles on APU-13 launch rails, and does not have the under-fuselage gun pod or pack, which was added to many EAF MiG-21PFM variants.

27

MiG-21FL (1411), 9th or 54th Sqn, SyAAF, location unknown, early 1970s
The most extreme versions of the 'tiger stripes' style of sand and spinach uppersurface camouflage seem to be found on Syrian MiG-21s, again reflecting the fact that they were applied locally. Here, however, the spinach has faded almost to brown. This aircraft participated in the October 1973 War, and is armed with R-3S missiles on APU-13 launch rails.

28

MiG-21bis (1487), SyAAF, unit and location unknown, 1982
The fact that this aircraft has the so-called 'Nile Valley' three-colour uppersurface camouflage scheme could indicate that it was originally built for sale to Egypt, but was then hurriedly delivered to Syria after relations between Egypt and the USSR deteriorated. It is armed with R-3R missiles beneath the outer underwing pylons, and pairs of R-60 missiles under APU-13 R-60 double launch-rails bolted to the inner underwing pylons. This aircraft probably took part in the fighting over Lebanon between 1979 and 1982.

29

MiG-21MF (2300), 5th Sqn, SyAAF, different locations (mainly Damascus area), 1973 to 1982
The two-colour uppersurface and sky blue undersides camouflage scheme on this aircraft is 'as delivered' from the Gorky factory in Russia. This proved very suitable over Syria, although it had not been so applicable to combat over Egypt. The aircraft is armed with R-3S missiles on APU-13 launch rails beneath the inner wing pylon and R-3R missiles on APU-13 launch-rails beneath the outer wing pylon. The centreline drop tank under the fuselage is painted the same sky blue as the aircraft's undersides. The serial number on the front fuselage is smaller than usual, and is still repeated in even smaller numerals above the fin-flash. This aircraft survived both wars. It was last noted – still in operational condition – in the late 1990s.

30

MiG-19S (660), 11th Sqn, IrAF, location unknown, circa 1963
This Iraqi aircraft is painted overall mid-grey and the serial number is repeated in small numerals on the underwing drop tanks, as was also seen on earlier MiGs in Egypt. The fin flash national markings used in 1962 and 1963 included three eight-pointed green outlined stars. There is no evidence that the names of Iraqi cities painted beneath the cockpits of MiG-19s transferred from

the Iraqi Air Force to the UARAF in the 1960s were also seen while the aircraft were still in Iraqi service. They were possibly added at the time of the transfer, or were perhaps applied to a different batch of MiG-19Ss

31

MiG-21F-13 (534), 17th Sqn, IrAF, H-3/al-Wallid, Iraq, 1966
This aircraft, belonging to the first IrAF unit to operate MiG-21s, was flown to Israel by Iraqi defector Capt Munir Radfa in 1966. It has the overall bare-metal finish seen on all Arab MiG-21s before the Six Day War. Note that the jet's serial was also repeated on the drop tank carried on the centreline.

32

MiG-21MF (681), 17th Sqn, IrAF, al-Hurriyah, near Kirkuk, Iraq, September 1980
The standard sand and spinach camouflage applied at factories in the Soviet Union included many variations in the basic pattern. This aircraft has a version with larger patches of dark green 'spinach' than usual. It is armed with R-3S missiles on APU-13 launch rails under the inboard underwing pylons, and carries bare-metal 490-litre drop tanks under the outboard under-wing pylons and another bare-metal 490-litre drop tank under the centreline pylon. This aircraft participated in the 1973 war with the 17th Sqn.

33

MiG-21MF (21178), probably 33rd Sqn, IrAF, Tallil, Iraq, 1991
This aircraft is reportedly from one of the last batches of MiG-21MFs delivered to Iraq. It was captured by US troops at Tallil in March 1991 and destroyed. Its uppersurface camouflage boasts only minimal spinach green patches, these having been applied in Gorky soon after construction. In the late 1980s many Iraqi MiG-21s were sent for refurbishment to Yugoslavia, which kept some examples back and replaced them with its own aircraft painted in a similar colour scheme, albeit with much wider patches and stripes. Note the new serial system introduced in 1987 and based on that used by the Yugoslav Air Force. It comprised five digits, of which the first two designated the aircraft type ('21' for MiG-21), the third the variant ('1' for MF) and the other two were individual aircraft serials. Of special interest on this aircraft is the application of a 'victory cockade' (to the right of the serial) which denoted an Iranian aircraft shot down by this machine sometime during the late 1980s.

34

F-7B (1511), 5th or 6th Sqn, IrAF, al-Ammarah or Karbala, Iraq, 1983
The 'sand and stone', or perhaps faded 'sand and spinach' uppersurface camouflage with sky blue undersides, was almost certainly applied after this aircraft was delivered to Iraq in early 1983. This

aircraft survived the war with Iran and was last seen in early 2003. A few Iraqi F-7Bs – probably those sent to Egypt for refurbishment in the late 1980s – were also painted in sand, spinach and brown.

35
MiG-21UM (21073), 29th or 33rd Sqn, IrAF, Tallil, Iraq, 1991

After surviving the long war with Iran, this aircraft was also captured by US forces at Tallil in 1991 and subsequently destroyed. Of special interest is the R-832 antenna in front of the fin, which was not seen very often on MiG-21UMs. During the latter stages of the war with Iran, special Iraqi strike package leaders are known to have used two-seaters as command and control aircraft when overseeing missions. The 'sand and stone' uppersurface and sky blue undersides camouflage on this aircraft were applied in Iraq. Note that the 490-litre centreline drop-tank has a bare metal finish.

COLOUR SECTION

1
This Egyptian MiG-21, serial number 8075, is a very unusual aircraft because it was either rebuilt from undamaged parts after the Six Day War or was extensively modified in Egypt. The basic machine is a MiG-21PFM with the brake 'chute fairing above the jet pipe partially replaced, or just unpainted. The tailfin, however, is of the narrower type, characteristic of a MiG-21F-13 or MiG-21PF. There also seem to have been repairs or modification to the fuselage spine, and the cockpit hood has been replaced. Finally, the jet's relatively fresh camouflage appears to be an early, perhaps experimental, version of the 'Nile Valley' scheme developed in Egypt in the early 1970s
(*Tom Cooper collection*)

2
A MiG-21MF in completely repainted Syrian Air Force markings and camouflage on display outside the 1973 War Panorama Museum in Damascus. The serial number 767 is painted in black outlined in white, which was never seen on machines actually in service. Furthermore, the SyAAF crest painted on the aircraft's nose was probably not applied to any operational aircraft either. The aircraft has R-3S air-to-air missiles beneath its inner underwing pylons, plus UB-16 unguided rocket-pods attached to the outer pylons
(*Tommy Vicard*)

3
One of 40 or so Chinese-built Shenyang F-6s purchased by the EAF. This upgraded version of the MiG-19S was armed with 30 mm cannon, and in Egyptian service the aircraft were also wired for AIM-9P Sidewinder missiles
(*Denis Hughes and AW&ST via Tom Cooper*)

4
A squadron line-up of EAF MiG-21s in the early 1980s, probably at Inshas. It includes, from left, a probable MiG-21FL or PFM, a MiG-21PFM (SPS) and a MiG-21PF, displaying two distinct versions of the 'sand and stone' camouflage schemes. Note that the furthest aircraft also has a new and as yet unpainted cockpit canopy frame
(*Lon Nordeen*)

5
An EAF F-7 is seen in a concrete hardened hanger at Fayid air base in 1989. The most obvious difference between the two types was the F-7's sideways opening cockpit canopy
(*Lon Nordeen*)

6
This battered Iraqi MiG-21PFMA, or possibly a MiG-21R (serial number 21302), was one of the few examples photographed by US troops during Operation *Desert Storm* prior to its destruction
(*US DoD*)

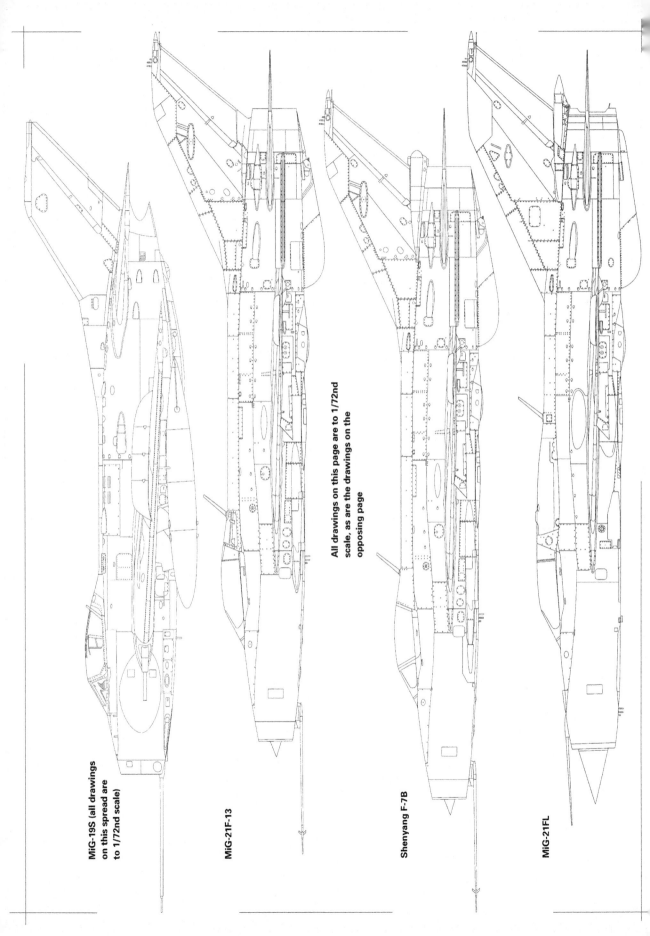

MiG-19S (all drawings on this spread are to 1/72nd scale)

MiG-21F-13

All drawings on this page are to 1/72nd scale, as are the drawings on the opposing page

Shenyang F-7B

MiG-21FL

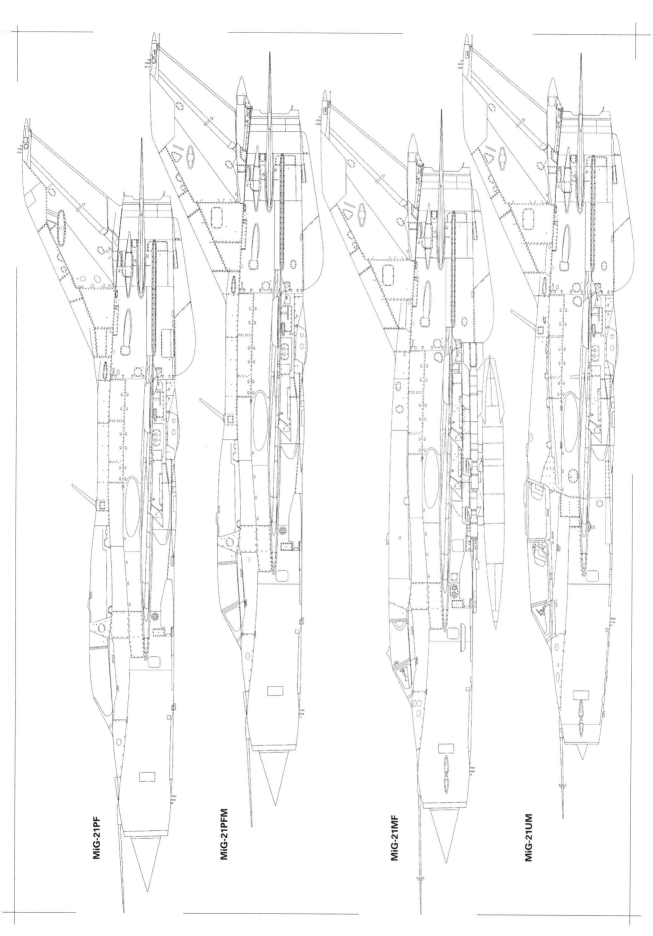

MiG-21PF

MiG-21PFM

MiG-21MF

MiG-21UM

INDEX